CLASSROOM DISCIPLINE
PROBLEM SOLVER

Ready-to-Use Techniques & Materials for Managing

All Kinds of Behavior Problems

CLASSROOM DISCIPLINE PROBLEM SOLVER

Ready-to-Use Techniques & Materials for Managing All Kinds of Behavior Problems

GEORGE WATSON

Illustrated by Alan Anthony

THE CENTER FOR APPLIED
RESEARCH IN EDUCATION
West Nyack, New York 10994

Library of Congress Cataloging-in-Publication Data

Watson, George.

   Classroom discipline problem solver : ready-to-use techniques &
materials for managing all kinds of behavior problems / George
Watson ; illustrated by Alan Anthony.

     p.   cm.

    ISBN 0-87628-134-X

    1. Classroom management—Handbooks, manuals, etc. 2. School
discipline—Handbooks, manuals, etc. I. Title.

  LB3013.W379   1998

  371.102'4—dc21
                              97-46411

                                  CIP

© 1998 *by* The Center for Applied Research in Education

Acquisitions Editor: *Connie Kallback*
Production Editor: *Tom Curtin*
Formatting/Interior Design: *Dee Coroneos*

Printed in the United States of America

10 9 8 7

ISBN 0-87628-134-X

**THE CENTER FOR APPLIED RESEARCH
IN EDUCATION**
West Nyack, NY 10994

On the World Wide Web at http://www.phdirect.com

DEDICATION

This book is dedicated to the following educators who, for some reason, had faith in me.

B. L. Korchinski—the principal who didn't listen to other people's judgments after I had failed grade 8 twice.

John Borycki—a man deserving profound respect, who was sensitive and caring during my last year of high school.

Len Donais—the Director of Education who gave me my first teaching position, September 2, 1973.

Ray Parent—my first principal, from whom I learned compassion, strength, consistency, and where the real values lie.

Steve Zurevinski—the best principal to have existed on the face of the earth.

Merv Grosse—the Director of Education who allowed me the stability and freedom to become an author.

Cam Gjosund—a Superintendent who encouraged me as well as contributed to this work.

ACKNOWLEDGMENTS

Judy Adair
Gene Aulinger
Ed Bath
Kelvin Bowers
Dorlas Bratvold
Lyle & Janice Brenna
Don Buglas
Barb Campbell
Adelard Carpentier
Bill Cowan
June Cubbon
Maxine Ekstrand
Audrey & Dennis Ens
Bill Flegel
Judy Fransoo
Jeff Gibson
Cam Gjosund
Merv Grosse
Carson Guenther
Karen Guenther
Matthew Guenther
John Hall
Greg Harnett
Rose Harnett
Irene & Pat Heffernan
Dave & Pat Holinaty
Pat Holuk
Esther Johnson
Don & Mary Johnston
Iris & Jack Jones
Terry Kjargaard

Shawn Kostiuk
Al Laughlin
Chad Lengyel
Evelyn Long
Leanne Markowsky
Judge William McCarroll
J. Vernon McGee
Ann Marie Merle
Al Monette
Myrna Nelson
Laurie Nyholt
Marie Parent
Elroy Peters
Ray Phaneuf
Denny Poulin
Hal Robinson
Randy Rodger
Brian Southgate
Treenie Sparling
Paul Stringer
Joanne Subchyshyn
Art & Joy Tegart
Diane & Jim Tiessen
Gord Waldner
Jake Wall
Christa Watson
Kathy Watson
Tony Watson
Amanda Weir
Amy Williams
Ann Marie Woytowich

vii

ABOUT THE AUTHOR

George Watson (B.A., University of Saskatchewan, Saskatoon, Saskatchewan, Canada) has taught almost every subject—including major academic subjects, physical education, and art—at the elementary and junior high school levels during twenty-four years of teaching. He currently teaches grades 8 and 9 and special education at Alexander Junior High School in the North Battleford (Saskatchewan) Public School Division. He has had short stories published in various Canadian magazines, as well as a book on hot rodding, and is the author of *Teacher Smart!* published by the Center for Applied Research in Education in 1996.

ABOUT THIS RESOURCE

Education cannot take place in an undisciplined environment. It is imperative that teachers maintain control of their classrooms if they are to be effective for the students and themselves. The problems of discipline must be solved by each and every teacher in each and every classroom.

In our modern culture, there are many new and varied pressures on teachers that did not exist even ten years ago. As a direct function of a changing value system, many of the parameters of discipline and control that once existed are no longer accepted. While the values of the culture are changing, some of the old problems teachers see in the schools are not. Problems of the school bully, vandalism, and swearing are, in fact, on the increase. In this environment, teachers need strong, tried-and-true techniques and guidelines in order to maintain proper working conditions. These very techniques and guidelines are provided in *Classroom Discipline Problem Solver*.

The tools, strategies, concepts, and ideas in this work are the result of intense research with a large number of successful teachers. These people have quality classroom management and discipline techniques. They have really enjoyed the profession for many years because of the control and order in their classrooms. These teachers have refined and developed their techniques in the crucible of the modern classroom by trial and error. In short, the hard work has already been done. Teachers need only read the various tactics or techniques to understand how they can be directly or indirectly adapted to the individual classroom.

Section 1, Techniques and Guidelines for Dealing with Fifty School Discipline Problems, leads the way in solving those classroom management and control issues we all face. "The Swearing Stopper" is a great example. With this idea, students are made to have ownership of the swearing problem as it occurs. They quickly realize that there will be larger consequences if there is a repeat performance.

Section 2, Problem-Solving Management Techniques That Keep Students on Task, offers techniques for a smoothly running classroom. Every teacher will agree that if the classroom has a calm, even flow, the discipline problems are at a minimum. One of the biggest difficulties teachers face is dealing with students who come to class unprepared; they disrupt the class to go to their lockers for materials and the teacher has to repeat information and instructions when they return. "The Class Parts Manager" offers the solution to this student problem, and includes a Materials Lent Out form to track both materials lent and students who are frequent offenders.

Discipline and solved problems can be the result of the proper use of reward and reinforcement systems. In Section 3, Positive Feelings and Creative Ideas, we develop this idea as many reinforcement and reward/management systems are offered. These, in effect, use positive feedback as a means of behavior regulation. The "Round 2-U" is a wonderful example of this. Instead of hassling with the student about due dates, the Round 2-U gives the student earned extra time to get his or her assignment "around to you," with no penalty and no problems. This works very well because teachers usually do not have enough time to grade a classroom load of reports, essays, and so on, in one day anyway. Included in Section 3 also (as the section heading suggests) are some things that are genuinely fun to do in school. They set the mood for the classroom as an enjoyable place to be.

In Section 4, Concepts That Protect and Techniques That Help, are solid ideas that help protect teachers, as well as students, in the ongoing classroom. "The Sitting Teddy" is a cute example of how you can protect younger students from potential embarrassment. It works great.

Section 5 is entitled Speak Easy—The Communication Section. Educators must be quality communicators, not only to transfer the curriculum to the students, but also to function in the interactive process of students, parents, colleagues, and administrators.

One of the many areas of communication that teachers must be adept at is getting the students to properly record and remember their homework assignments. The "Assignment Notepad" is dandy for solving problems in this area. With this, all the students carry a small notepad from class to class. They write their assignments in the pad to remind them of what they are to do for homework. The parents are informed of this and can look at their son's or daughter's notepad each day as it is brought home. No longer will parents ask their children, "Do you have any homework tonight?" The parents need only look at the notepad to see what has to be done. It is always nice to see a single idea put to good use solving problems.

Classroom Discipline Problem Solver is a 100 percent benefit for teachers. Ideas in this resource help to create that disciplined environment we all need. The techniques, strategies, and concepts were chosen because they were very practical. They are easy to use and are low cost. Some have great detail, others are simple, but they all have one thing in common—they work.

CONTENTS

About This Resource. ix

Section One

TECHNIQUES AND GUIDELINES FOR DEALING WITH 50 SCHOOL DISCIPLINE PROBLEMS

1 The Fifty Rules of Classroom Discipline. 3

2 The Swearing Stopper. 7

   1-1 Inappropriate Language Form / 8

3 Guidelines for Dealing with Foul Language at School 9

4 Seven Ways to Avoid Problems Over Students' Marks 10

5 Five Ways to Quiet the Class Quickly. 11

6 Five Ways to Minimize the Talking Problem 13

7 Five-Card Talk Control 14

8 Drugs—The Bane of Society 15

9 How a Successful Work Experience Program Functions and Solves
   Problems 17

   1-2 Work Experience Program Agreement and Consent Form / 20

   1-3 Teacher/Employer Contact Sheet / 21

   1-4 Student Worker Evaluation Sheet / 22

10 Solid Concepts on Seven Areas of Teaching—Communicating
    Directly. 23

11 Guidelines for a Problem-Free Museum or Art Gallery Field Trip. 26

12 Solving Problems for the Do-Nothing, Unmotivated, Apathetic Student 28

13 Understanding Peer Influences 30

14 It's a Seedy Thing to Do 32

    1-5 This Is a NO Sunflower Seed Zone / 33

15 How to Deal with the Discipline Problems of Bright, High-Performance Students and the Parents of Those Students 34

16 Guidelines for Dealing with Sexual Harassment Anywhere in the School Environment 36

17 The Five-Step Problem Solver 38

    1-6 The Five-Step Problem Solver Form / 40

18 Mike's Story 41

19 Guidelines for Dealing with the School Bully 43

20 Desk Discipline 45

    1-7 Your Desk Is a Disaster / 46

21 Guidelines for Dealing with Vandalism 47

22 Verbal Abuse Guidelines 49

23 The Attendance Concentration Idea 51

24 Two Ways to Resolve a Minor Student Dispute 52

    1-8 Dispute Sheet / 53

25 The Behavior Station Program 54

    1-9 Concern Level One—Behavior Description Sheet / 56
    1-10 Concern Level Two—Behavior Knowledge Sheet / 57
    1-11 Concern Level Three (Final)—Behavior Results Sheet / 58

26 Solving Problems Before, During, and After the School Dance 59

27 The Behavior Control Ticket 61

    1-12 Behavior Control Tickets / 62

28 Hallway and Washroom Problem Solvers 63

1-13 Hall and Washroom Sign / 64

29 Seating Plan Manipulation 65

30 Guidelines for Dealing with Students with Short Attention Spans 66

31 Eighteen Ways to Prevent Theft in School 67

32 Helping the Student Who Is Always Late 69

1-14 Admit to Class / 71

33 Avoiding Problems on the First Day of School 72

34 The Five Greatest Fears or Concerns of Parents 73

35 Fifty Suicide Indicators—Symptoms and Insights 75

36 Guidelines for Dealing with Students Who Skip School
(An Attendance Policy) 78

37 How to Have a Productive Meeting with the Parents of a
Behavior-Problem Child 80

38 Guidelines for Dealing with Bomb Threats 81

39 The Junior Janitor Program 83

40 The Student Connection Process—A Teacher-to-Office
Communication, Support, and Discipline System 84

1-15 Quick Details Form / 86
1-16 Student Connection Form / 87

41 What to Do and What Not to Do When You See a Person with
a Gun in School 89

42 The Thirty-Five Minute Solution 91

43 The Project Shop (a Unique, Yet Effective, Behavior-Control Idea) . . . 92

44 Guidelines for Dealing with Fights at School 93

45 What to Do When You Are Physically Attacked by a Student 95

46 Seven Ways to Make Sure Homework Gets Completed 97

47 Dealing with the Back-Talking Student 98

48 Guidelines for Dealing with a Challenging Parent. 100

49 Self-Discipline Guidelines for Teachers. 101

50 Fifty Ways to Discourage and Prevent Cheating in the Classroom. . . . 103

Section Two
PROBLEM-SOLVING MANAGEMENT TECHNIQUES
THAT KEEP STUDENTS ON TASK

51 The Job Jar and Fifty Jobs. 109

52 The Track and Field or Sports Day Problem Solver. 112

   2-1 Track and Field Meet Schedule / 114

53 The Name Game—A Memory Enhancer. 115

54 Sandpaper Letters 116

55 Level Grouping for Maximum Learning. 117

56 The Class Parts Manager 118

   2-2 Materials Lent Out / 120

57 Timer Controls 121

58 The Twelve Big Don'ts of Teaching. 122

59 Shared Writing 123

60 The Desk Pak Storage Problem Solver. 125

61 Stump the Experts. 127

62 The Old-Fashioned Spelling Bee 129

63 The New-Fashioned Spelling Bee 130

64   The Best Book Report Form in the Business   132

     2-3 The Book Report Form / 133

65   The Monthly Seating Plan Rotation System   134

66   The Instant Newspaper Assignment Form   135

     2-4 The Instant Newspaper Assignment Form / 136

67   The Who, What, When, Where, Why, and How of It All—
    A Lesson in Continuity   137

     2-5 Story Elements Sheet / 139

68   Charades—A Terrific Tool   140

69   Wonderfully Unique Ideas of Merit   141

70   Number Control   143

71   Two Ways to Use Colors to Solve Problems   144

72   The Animal Spelling Chart   145

73   The High Five Classroom Controller   146

74   The Mini Debate   147

75   The Ten Most Important Test-Writing Skills   148

76   Role-Playing   150

Section Three

POSITIVE FEELINGS AND CREATIVE IDEAS

77   The Penny Carnival and Fifty Great Ideas to Help Make It
    a Success   155

78   Totally Neat Pun Tickets   159

     3-1 Pun Tickets / 160

79   Free-from-Homework Cards   162

     3-2 Free-from-Homework Card / 163

80 The Round 2-U 164
   3-3 *Round 2-U / 165*

81 Behavior Bucks 166
   3-4 *Behavior Bucks / 167*

82 The Twenty-Five-Space Card System 168
   3-5 *The 25-Space Card Form / 169*

83 The Double Diamond Awards 170
   3-6 *Double Diamond Award / 171*

84 The Environmental Award—Solving Larger Problems 172
   3-7 *The Environmental Award Application Form / 173*

85 Posi-Notes—A Good Thing; Cheap Too! 174
   3-8 *Positive Note Forms / 175*

86 The Pro-Merit System 176

87 Earned Five-Minute Free-Time Cards 178
   3-9 *Five-Minute Free-Time Card / 179*

88 The Nut-and-Bolt Reward System 180

89 The Pot O' Gold, Dirt Dessert, Environmentally Friendly Idea 182

90 Switch a Kid 183

91 One-Break Cards 184
   3-10 *One-Break Card / 185*

92 Positive Speak 186

Section Four
CONCEPTS THAT PROTECT AND TECHNIQUES THAT HELP

93 Fifty Strategies and Survival Guidelines for the First-
Year Teacher 191

94   Sticky Labels—Records on the Wrist............................   195

95   The Dewey Decimal Book Organizer Bingo...................   196

96   The Friendship Club...   197

97   The Sitting Teddy..   198

98   Up-Front Assignment Chart.....................................   199
     4-1 Up-Front Assignment Chart / 201

99   String Along with Me..   202

100 The Plot Chart and Plot Dice...................................   203
     4-2 Creative Writing Plot Chart / 205

101 Volunteers—Wonderful Helpers...............................   206
     4-3 Volunteer Contract / 207
     4-4 Volunteer Log Sheet / 208

102 The Point Target Sheet...   209
     4-5 Sample Point Target Sheet / 210

103 The Value of CPR and First-Aid Training for Teachers...   211

104 The Notebook Check and Grade Sheet........................   212
     4-6 Notebook Check and Grade Sheet / 213

105 Portfolios or Document Folders................................   214

106 Protect Yourself—Read This....................................   216
     4-7 Incident Flowchart / 217

107 The Community Service Program...............................   218

108 How a Camera Can Assist in the Discipline and PR Process...   219

109 The Anecdotal Protection System.............................   220
     4-8 Anecdotal Record Form / 221

110 The Paradigm Expansion Chart.................................. 222

    4-9 The Paradigm Expansion Chart / 223

111 The Custodial Staff—Problem Solvers for You 224

Section Five
SPEAK EASY—THE COMMUNICATION SECTION

112 Fifty Communication Tips for Teachers 229

113 The Class Diary... 234

    5-1 Class Diary Form / 235

114 The Post Office Management System........................... 236

115 Assignment Notepads.. 237

116 Teacher-to-Parent Data Communication Form................. 238

    5-2 Teacher-to-Parent Data Communication Form / 239

117 The Missed-Assignment Binder............................... 240

    5-3 Missed-Assignment Sheet / 241

118 Anomie—A Teacher Problem 242

119 The Sign-Out Sheet.. 243

    5-4 Sign-Out Sheet / 244

120 Foreign Relations 245

121 The Report Card Memo....................................... 246

    5-5 Report Card Memo / 247

    5-6 Report Card Memo (variation) / 248

122 The Pros and Cons of Eleven Different Evaluation Systems......... 249

123 The Fear-of-Public-Speaking Problem Solver 253

124 Two Daily Notice or Bulletin Systems for Quick Communication.... 255

125 The Comprehensive Contract 256

     5-7 A Sample of a Comprehensive Contract / 257

126 The Youth Court Solution 258

127 Posi-Calls 260

     5-8 Positive Call Record Sheet / 261

Section One

TECHNIQUES AND GUIDELINES FOR DEALING WITH 50 SCHOOL DISCIPLINE PROBLEMS

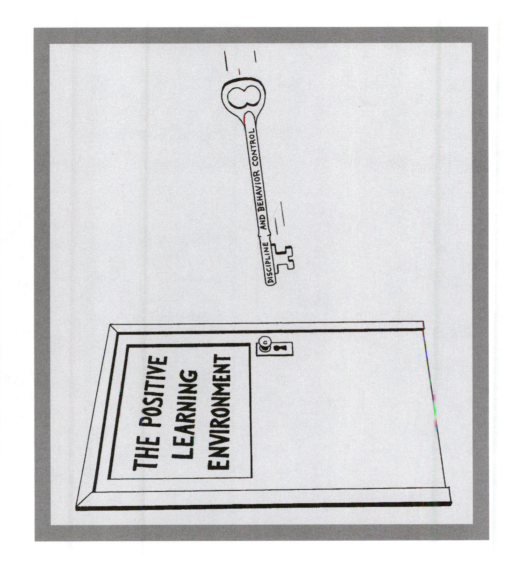

Every teacher needs control in her or his classroom. This is fundamental to creating a positive learning environment for students.

Discipline and management techniques can be developed through the hit-and-miss process of experience or they can be learned from reading the information researched from many successful educators. This is the knowledge we present in Section 1.

These fifty strategies have survived the test of time and hard knocks. They have had their rough edges sheared off in the refining process of the classroom. Here you will find ideas that work.

THE FIFTY RULES OF CLASSROOM DISCIPLINE

Certain fundamental rules of classroom discipline, developed over the ages, have validity in almost every working classroom in the world. It is important, therefore, that all teachers know and adhere to these basic rules if they are to create a positive learning environment for their students.

Both students and parents appreciate a classroom that is well managed. The properly controlled classroom gives a feeling of security and comfortable predictability to everyone. Even the most insecure student should be able to grow and mature in the strong, unbiased—yet gentle and compassionate—atmosphere of your classroom.

The following fifty rules will help you develop that positive learning environment.

1. Start the year off with a thought-out discipline plan. Spend some time before school begins to go over those discipline procedures that work. Plan to use new ideas as you come across them. Keep a record of what works best at this time of year.

2. Do not leave your classroom unattended. Try to be in the classroom when students arrive.

3. Be reliable and consistent. If you say you are going to do something, then carry it through.

4. Respect every student. Rules and written guidelines for conduct can never take the place of mutual respect.

5. Do not ignore poor behavior.

6. Do not favor one student over another. Watch that you do not create a "teacher's pet."

7. Do not put a jackknife or other tool on your school key ring. Students can use these as offensive weapons. You will get all or part of the blame.

8. Do not allow a student to hide behind a bookcase or larger student.

9. Seek interactive support from the school office.

10. Choose judiciously which demands of your students you will support.

11. Use your voice to control behavior. Develop a strong, resolute tone that the students will recognize.

12. Organize your classroom to control behavior. Separate peers and have a consistent seating plan. Do not allow grouping of desks in one corner.

13. Show zero tolerance for put-downs in your classroom.

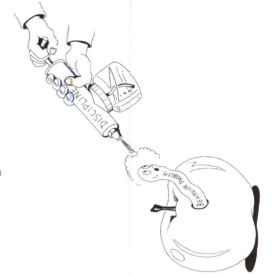

14. Do not try to speak over the students' talking. Do not try to drown the students out. Quiet them down before speaking.

15. Develop a routine for dealing with the students; for example, to ask or answer questions, students must put their hands up. If you do not use this routine, the question-and-answer process will quickly deteriorate into a blurting session, with students responding at inappropriate times and in an inappropriate manner.

16. Lock up any chemicals or sharp objects.

17. Have 100 percent supervision when dealing with anything hot.

18. Show zero tolerance for abusive behavior. The theme of respect for self, others, and property should be adopted.

19. Seat behavior problems and potential behavior problems around your desk.

20. Keep behavior problems and potential behavior problems busy 100 percent of the time.

21. If a student from another class comes to your classroom door asking to speak to a student, find out if it is an emergency. If not, then do not allow the person at the door to disrupt your class further by talking to the student he or she has asked for.

22. Show zero tolerance for water pistols, elastic bands, pea or spitball shooters, and so forth.

23. Do not place students in the hall, out of your sight, to do work.

24. Show zero tolerance for swearing or foul language in your classroom.

25. Show zero tolerance for note passing.

26. Make your classroom a "junk-food-free zone." This includes gum, candy, and potato-based chip products. Some students may react negatively to sugar and other chemicals (e.g., MSG) in junk food.

27. Expect to be tested by the students. They will push you as far as they can to define the limits of their behavior with you.

28. If you are called into judgment because of a dispute or a disciplinary matter and it looks serious, watch what you say. Call your professional association immediately.

29. Do not go on field trips without competent extra help. This extra help must have the skills and authority to maintain discipline.

30. One of the greatest disciplinary tools of all on field trips is the cellular phone. If behavior or other problems arise, you can contact the school, parents, or anyone else—for example, the police—needed to help you.

31. Try to hone your automatic management skills. These allow you to react almost instantly with the proper response to a behavior problem, decision-making situation, or improper noise level.

32. If a group of students enters your classroom in a loud boisterous mood, you must calm them down. Tell them to put their heads on the desk in front of them. This will relax the students and reduce the noise level.

33. The sanction you mete out must be equal to the transgression.

4

34. If you must ask for help from the school office on a "very often" basis, you had better reassess your discipline strategy.

35. Detention rooms and separate school suspension areas have been challenged in the courts and are now disallowed in many jurisdictions.

36. If you have a sanction for a particular offense (e.g., swearing) given to one person, the next time you catch someone else with the same behavior, you must administer the same sanction.

37. When correcting tests while students are in the class, do not return them one by one as they are corrected. Finish the entire set of tests, then give them back to the students. If you return them as they are completed one by one, this in itself will disturb the class.

38. If a problem occurred in the morning, it should be dealt with then. Resolution of the problem is less effective if you delay responding until later in the day.

39. If behavior control is not adequate in the school hallways, this will be reflected in student conduct as they enter the classrooms.

40. Corporal punishment is usually not effective on the person you administer it to. It does, however, have a detrimental, frightening effect on everyone else in the class. A classroom based on fear is not a positive learning environment. Corporal punishment is being challenged in the courts and is being disallowed by many schools.

41. Always remember, a big problem today between two students, quite likely will not exist tomorrow.

42. Do not forget the five components of school rules. School rules must:

    a. be fair
    b. be consistent
    c. respect rights and privileges
    d. be understandable
    e. be workable

43. The best classroom discipline occurs when you have detailed working knowledge of your students. Always keep in mind that a lot of children today are carrying social-emotional baggage.

44. Remember that people will act and react differently when in a group than when they are alone. Discipline techniques that may work when Johnny is alone may not work when he is with his friends.

45. The classrooms of today are multi-ethnic in makeup. It is important for the modern teacher to develop a sensitivity to the customs and cultural diversity of the students and their families. Discipline techniques may have to be adjusted accordingly.

46. The more organized you are, the better your discipline will be.

47. The more enthusiastic you are, the more enthusiastic the students will be. This will lead to better classroom management.

48. Show zero tolerance for items or substances that can irritate or have the potential to injure. These include itching powders, sneezing powder, or stink-bomb substances.

49. Do not expose your coffee cup in the classroom where students can add something to it.

50. While there should be generally agreed-upon discipline policies in every school, you, as the individual teacher, cannot expect the teacher down the hall to have the same conduct expectations that you have.

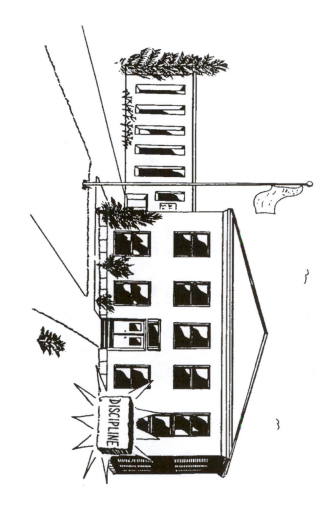

6

THE SWEARING STOPPER

Some students will use foul or abusive language in school. This inappropriate behavior is often a function of the student's subculture and should not be tolerated by staff and other students.

How can you teach students that swearing and foul language are not acceptable in the social circumstance of the school? How can you develop in students the social skill of using proper language in the proper place?

Use the Swearing Stopper idea to solve this problem. When you hear a student cursing or swearing, make the student write down on the Inappropriate Language Form (Figure 1-1) exactly what he or she said. No detail should be left out. The student is also to write on the form the exact circumstances that led up to or caused the foul language to occur.

Either the principal or teacher takes the Inappropriate Language Form, adds the proper comments, seals it in an envelope that has the school's logo on it, and writes the address of the parent on the envelope as the student watches. The school official then affixes a stamp to the envelope and pins the letter onto the bulletin board in his or her office.

At this point, the student is told, "If we have one more incident of your using foul language in school, I am going to take this letter off the bulletin board and mail it to your parents."

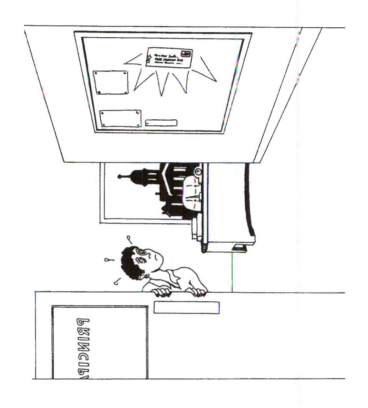

This idea works beautifully. The student will have a perpetual consciousness that the letter, in her or his own handwriting, will end up at his or her parent's house.

In fact, students whose letters have been placed on the principal's or teacher's bulletin board have often been observed craning their necks to see if their letter is still in place on that board.

Figure 1-1

Inappropriate Language Form

Name: _____   Date: _____

Describe in detail what you said. Leave nothing out. _____

_____

_____

_____

Describe the circumstance that caused you to use inappropriate language.

_____

_____

_____

_____
Student Signature

Principal/Teacher's Comments: _____

_____

_____

_____
Principal's/Teacher's Signature

3

GUIDELINES FOR DEALING WITH FOUL LANGUAGE AT SCHOOL

One of the major problems teachers have to endure in today's schools is the fact that many children curse, swear, or use foul language. Educators will tell you they are seeing this problem at earlier and earlier age levels. The problem of foul language is often a direct function of its use in many homes.

Swearing, cursing, and other foul language, including racial slurs, must not be seen to be tolerated even to the slightest degree. If you merely give lip service to resolving the problem, you will degrade your own work environment and therefore increase your own stress by having to listen to it.

Here are some guidelines for dealing with the problem of foul language in the school:

1. Create a zero tolerance policy in your school for any swear word, cursing, or racial slur.

2. If an example occurs in your classroom, don't overreact by getting angry or hostile. This first time is often a shot to test your level of tolerance. Deal with the problem by turning the situation into a learning experience about foul language—who is hurt by it, why people are insulted by it, and so on. (Put lots of notes on the board on this topic for the students to copy.)

3. Many students who use foul language are just plain ignorant of the meaning of what they are saying. If you explain the meaning of the swear words to them (especially the younger set), it is most likely they will think twice before using the bad words again.

4. Quite often, children who swear or curse in school do not have any other way to express their frustration. Again, education is the key here. Teach the child to have a more socially accepted method of expressing his or her feelings.

5. Recognize that some students are immature and will want to identify with peers or siblings and therefore will use foul language as a means of identifying with a group.

6. Some students will swear simply to get attention. There are, however, some students who are looking to get a strong negative reaction out of you. They sometimes do this to impress their peers. Don't play into this power game.

7. Many students in school have strong religious beliefs and standards. If some other student curses their God, it is seen as an invasion of the rights and freedoms of the religious person. That religious person's rights must be respected.

8. Foul language need not be defined only as swearing, cursing, or racial slurs. Perhaps some of the cruelest foul language of all is that which puts down or hurts other people—language that mocks physical or mental disabilities or degrades anyone.

SEVEN WAYS TO AVOID PROBLEMS OVER STUDENTS' MARKS

Many students are intensely competitive, especially when it comes to school grades or marks. Much of the competitiveness is self-directed and self-motivating. There is basically nothing wrong with this as long as the drive and the behaviors related to it are healthy and honest.

Competitiveness becomes a problem when students or parents want to outperform some other person or group not for the sake of personal growth but to win at all costs. Other students find some kind of pleasure in knowing and broadcasting that somebody else did not do as well as they did on a particular test. This goes beyond competitiveness; it is pure spite. These attitudes can cause you trouble when it comes to mark distribution and grade records.

The following set of guidelines can help you avoid some of those very real problems associated with student marks.

1. Do not post student marks unless names are coded by a student number system.

2. Do not have so many bonus points that a student's average grade exceeds 100 percent.

3. When a parent tells you that another student is not as good as his or her child, do not let this become a self-fulfilling prophecy when grading essays and other papers.

4. Do not have one student hand out graded tests, especially if the score on the tests is right on the front. You must hand out each paper.

5. Some students sitting near you will have telescopic vision when you are marking tests at your desk. Avoid prying eyes when you mark or grade work.

6. Do not leave your mark book on your desk.

7. Do not distribute tests to other students for them to correct each other's paper. This may be quick, but it certainly is not efficient. Students tend to miss answers or mark incorrect responses as correct—intentionally or unintentionally.

FIVE WAYS TO QUIET THE CLASS QUICKLY

One of the problems you will have when you enter almost any classroom is that the students will be talking. Even the quietest students will have something to say to someone. Quite often, talking has the momentum of a forest fire; it creates its own wind. This makes it difficult to reduce the noise level as you enter the class. Do not add to the noise level; it just increases your stress.

The following five no-stress successful techniques will instantly quiet the class down so you can teach.

1. Train the students to respond to the arm-in-the-air technique. Simply put your arm in the air with your hand open and instruct the students to do the same. They are to stop talking as soon as they see your hand go up or another student's hand being raised. This works very well, even when a student is turned around or looking sideways. That student will see the people beside or behind him or her with their hands up and immediately know the classroom is to be quiet.

2. Stand in front of the students and start counting sternly—1, 2, 3, and so on. You won't get to 7 before they will all have quieted down.

3. Have an instant assignment on the board for students to work on as they walk into class. Tell the students that assignment is worth five points (how you apply them is at your discretion) or it is worth percentage points for the in-class behavior or work-skills section of their report cards. Design the assignment to be corrected right away, thus adding to the urgency of the work. This really works, and it sets the tone for the rest of that period.

4. When you walk into a noisy class, tell students to quickly put their fingers on their noses; all will stop talking to do this. Then you start the lesson. Likewise, if you tell the students to hold their breath instantly, they will have to stop talking to do this.

5. Develop the red, white, and blue dot system. This requires some training and instruction prior to implementation. Inform the students that there are three levels of sound allowed in your classroom, and these are indicated by the three colored dots. You will indicate what noise level you will tolerate by what color of dot is taped on the chalkboard. Tell the students that if they see a red dot on the board, they will know they are not to talk at all under any circumstances. If they see a white dot, they are allowed to talk to get work or an assignment completed with a low-to-medium noise level. If they see a blue dot, it means the students may talk freely and have a normal conversational sound level in the class.

It will take some training and practice before an average class knows how to respond to the colored dots the way you want them to. Your diligence in this training will make the system work.

Once the system is operational, reducing the noise level in the classroom becomes easy for you. You just walk in, take a dot and put it up on the chalkboard or bulletin board. You will not have to say a word or in any way stress yourself out in order to quickly quiet the classroom.

12

FIVE WAYS TO MINIMIZE THE TALKING PROBLEM

Teachers work hard preparing lessons. When you present the material, you want students to be attentive throughout the whole presentation. There is the rub. It does not always happen. Some students will not have the same degree of appreciation for the material as you, and they will begin to talk.

The problem for teachers since the dawn of antiquity has been—how do you stop or prevent students from talking while you are making a presentation?

There are obvious things to do, like telling the students to quit talking or removing a student from the classroom. These we don't deal with; you find here five basic ideas that are strong and successful, and will have long-term results.

Five Ways to Minimize the Talking Problem:

1. Separate peers. Move friends from the vicinity of one another. You can use proximity of peers as a reward. If students are quiet, they can return to the area of their friends; if not, they stay separated.

2. The direct silent eye. This is a specific technique that requires you to look directly at the student talking with a cold, hard stare. Once the student notices, you do not say a word but continue with your lesson. It takes a while to perfect the technique, but it is one of the most effective talking control mechanisms in the business.

3. Some students are chronic talkers. With this type of student, you must use a reward system like "Keep a Reward Cards." Give the chronic talker four cards that have a different no-cost reward written on them (e.g., wear a hat in school). Tell the student it is up to him or her to try to keep the reward cards that are redeemable at the end of the month (or week). They can keep the reward cards by not talking during class.

   Every time the chronic talker talks or disturbs you, remove a card from him or her. Make sure you leave the most prized reward for the last.

4. When teaching a skill subject like math at the board, it is important to keep the students on their toes in order to minimize the possibility of talking and misbehavior. This is accomplished by pointing to specific students in the ongoing process of instruction and asking them this question, "Judy, would you be able to explain this back to me?" The process of asking this question of different individuals keeps them all on their toes because they do not know who will be asked next. The question must be asked sporadically, so students cannot predict your pattern.

5. Make your lessons interactive. This means the students will have an assignment to do as you are presenting the lesson. They will not have time to talk because of their need to pick up answers from you as you speak.

13

FIVE-CARD TALK CONTROL

Are you looking for a quick, easy-to-use and effective method to stop the habitual talker in your classroom? The five-card talking control idea is the answer.

How It Works

1. Make five colorful cards about the size of playing cards. Put big, bold numbers on the cards from one to five.

2. Explain to the students that these are talking control cards. All five cards will be given to the person who needs to stop his or her inappropriate talking.

3. Inform the students that you will remove one card from the person each time he or she talks out of turn or at an inappropriate time. The consequence for a student's having all five cards removed is at your discretion, but it must be meaningful.

4. Once you have identified the student who needs the talking control, give him or her the cards, but immediately take away card number one. Tell the student that this first card was removed because of the talking that occurred now.

5. You will find that you need to remove only one or two cards from the talking student in order to quiet him or her down. The cards on the desk serve to remind the student that he or she has been targeted for discipline. They allow the student some leeway to get a grip on his or her behavior before that disciplinary action must be taken. It is wonderful to see a simple idea that works so well, is easy to implement, and costs nothing.

DRUGS—THE BANE OF SOCIETY

The use of illicit drugs by teenagers has been a fiercely growing problem since the "hippie" days of the 1960s and 1970s. Schools have had to deal with every imaginable type and effect of prescription and nonprescription substances. Educators, counselors, and medical staff cannot understand why perfectly normal, well-adjusted young people would risk their health for the sake of getting high on some unknown chemical.

One fundamental reason students or young people do drugs is because they live basically for the moment. Quite a few do not have the ability from experience to predict long-term consequences of actions, and if they see that drugs can affect them in the future, they often don't care. The current thrill of the high is all-encompassing.

It therefore falls upon those who deal and work with young people to break through that mindset to connect with young people and educate them on this issue—a sometimes difficult thing to do. The following are some things the school can do to solve problems in this area:

1. Promote a zero tolerance policy for drugs and alcohol.

2. If you suspect illicit drugs are in a student's locker or desk, bring in the drug-sniffing dog to confirm this. If it is legal in your jurisdiction, open the student's locker and have the student arrested immediately if drugs are found.

3. Tell recess and noon hour supervisors to be on the lookout for strangers talking to students in the schoolyard or adjacent to it.

4. Disallow beepers (pagers) in your school—they are used by drug dealers to inform students when a shipment comes in. They also disrupt the class during lessons.

5. Some students may be at risk from their parents. If possible, identify these people through the school guidance office or school counselor. Seek professional help for these people.

6. Develop a "tips" hot line for information leading to the arrest of persons possessing or dealing in drugs.

7. Educational antidrug programs should begin at the kindergarten level and continue into the last days of high school. They should be part of the curriculum at every grade level.

8. If you suspect a student of possessing drugs, give him or her a chance to "come clean" by asking this question, "Is there anything you want to tell me or give me?" By this question, you are not accusing the student of possessing drugs; you are, in effect, giving the student a chance to confess and often the student will take it.

9. Encourage parents to keep their children involved in school and community programs. Students who participate in a band program, for example, have a physical and mental perspective from which to feel good about themselves. A student who has a positive personal sense of self-worth is less likely to do drugs.

10. Develop a no-drug safety zone for the two-block area around your school. This program must be coordinated with the local police, who will arrange to have signs installed, indicating the zone. As part of that no-drug safety zone, penalties for any drug offense in that area should be at least twice the normal rate.

11. Sponsor programs like SADD (Students Against Drunk Driving). These groups heighten awareness of the problem and are often instrumental in keeping drunk or high students (and others) off the streets and highways.

12. Watch for drugs or alcohol on field, sports, or band trips. Have parents and students sign a no-drugs-or-alcohol form before they leave. If a prohibited substance is found in the possession of a student, there should be a provision to send or bring that child home immediately.

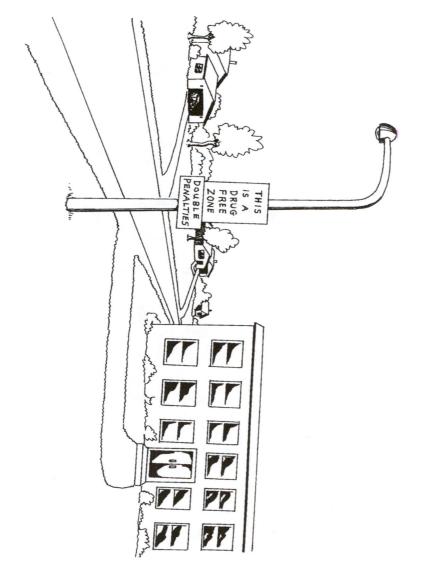

16

HOW A SUCCESSFUL WORK EXPERIENCE PROGRAM FUNCTIONS AND SOLVES PROBLEMS

In all of education, a few programs are worth their weight in gold when it comes to helping students be gainfully employed. The work experience program is truly one of these. Under this program, students are placed at cooperating businesses in the school's community to enhance their education with work-related skills.

The student is placed at a job station for one basic reason—to learn the necessary job skills that will allow him or her to become a worker at some future date in that field or profession. Students may work in an auto body repair shop, for example, with the idea of entering that field immediately after finishing their high school years. Some students may be placed at a career location that requires a number of years of post-secondary training to be qualified for—for example, working in a veterinary clinic.

In this latter case, the student is placed there to see if the profession is suitable for him or her before entering years of training for it. Learning you do not like a job or profession before you educate yourself for it is valuable indeed.

How a Successful Work Experience Functions

1. You must offer pre-employment preparation for the student. This preparation should include:

   ⬆ Consultation with the student regarding interest, as well as when he or she would like to be placed.

   ⬆ Job expectations of the student and the employer as to the nature of the job.

   ⬆ Coaching on interpersonal skills—how to get along on the job.

   ⬆ Check of transportation availability.

   ⬆ Safety procedures on the job.

   ⬆ What is covered by insurance.

   ⬆ How to manage time at breaks and lunch.

   ⬆ Conforming to the work station dress code.

   ⬆ Hours of work—punctuality.

   ⬆ Being a self-starter—not having to be told to do everything.

2. It is not a good idea to place students at a job site or work station before the age of 14. The maturity to learn work skills is sometimes not in place before this age. There may be age restrictions in your jurisdiction. This must be checked out.

3. All paperwork including the Work Experience Program Agreement and Consent Form (Figure 1-2) must be completed by the student and his or her parents prior to job placement.

4. The work stations themselves must be set up through old-fashioned legwork, by calling upon potential businesses and institutions that would be able to support your program. Employers should be given a fact sheet stating your expectations and their responsibilities.

17

5. Once the teacher/supervisor has prepared a student, the supervisor will take the student to the desired work station and introduce her or him to the work station boss or the management person at that location.

6. When the student is introduced to the employer, all parties must sign a Work Placement Agreement. This document must be drawn up specifically for your jurisdiction by a lawyer. The agreement must cover general work procedures, expectations, liability, and what to do in case of injury to the student. The amount of insurance the school system carries regarding this program should be stated in this Work Placement Agreement.

7. Students work at a job site in a time frame that will allow them to keep up with their academic work. Three popular patterns are: one full day or afternoon a week, every afternoon or morning five days a week, or two and a half days each week.

8. Students are to understand that they are there to learn to be workers and are not to receive or expect any financial remuneration for their work during school hours. If a student is hired by the employer after school or on weekends, that arrangement is between the student and the employer and is not a concern of the supervisor or the school.

9. When necessary, students will be moved from one work station to another. This move will be agreed upon by the student and the teacher/supervisor.

10. If there is a conflict or poor performance on the part of a student, every effort to rectify the situation will be made by the supervisor, the student, and the employer. If this cannot be accomplished, the student will be removed from that work station.

11. The teacher/supervisor will visit or telephone each work station or job site on a regular basis. He or she will complete the necessary section of the Teacher/Employer Contact Sheet (Figure 1-3).

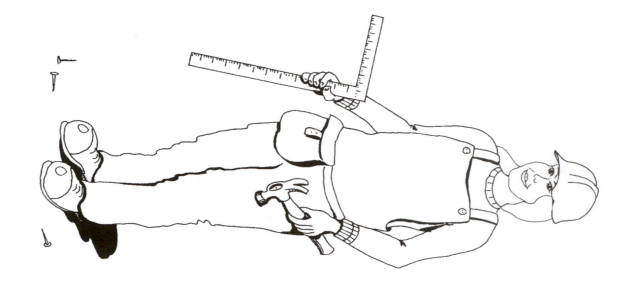

18

12. The students will receive evaluations from the teacher/supervisor at regular intervals.

13. The employer will complete the Student Worker Evaluation Sheet (Figure 1-4) when the teacher/supervisor designates.

14. Under no circumstances is the student worker to take the place of any regular employee or to be seen as taking the place of any regular employee at any time.

15. When Awards Night occurs at your school, have a trophy or certificate for the student worker with the best record of performance.

16. Following are the five important behavioral objectives for Students in Work Experience Programs:

    a. To develop an appreciation of the employer-employee relationship

    b. To develop a positive working relationship with other employees

    c. To appreciate the need for leadership in the work setting

    d. To appreciate the dynamics of employee-customer relationships

    e. To develop an understanding of the transfer of academic skills to the job site

Figure 1-2

WORK EXPERIENCE PROGRAM AGREEMENT AND CONSENT FORM

I hereby give my complete permission to enroll my child, _____, in the Work Training Program.

I understand that:

(a)   This is a training program designed to prepare my child to become a worker rather than to train for a specific job.

(b)   My child may have several placements, over a period of time, with cooperating employers.

(c)   My child will have periodic supervision by school supervisory personnel while on the job.

(d)   Where a medical certificate is required for work experience, it will be made available to the employer.

(e)   The program includes various tests and assessments, by both in-school and out-of-school professionals. As parent or guardian, I give my permission for this to be completed as required.

(f)   It is the parent's or guardian's responsibility to notify the supervisor at work and the teacher when the student is going to be absent.

(g)   When my child is required to leave the work station during work hours, for whatever reason, I will be sure to provide the employer with written communication or a phone call.

(h)   Liability insurance coverage for my child is provided by the school jurisdiction.

(i)   I understand that my child is not eligible to receive pay while in training.

(j)   I will encourage my child to be honest, punctual, and polite at all times.

(k)   Whenever I have any concerns about the program, I will channel my communication through the principal and teacher supervisor at the school.

(l)   If selected for the Work Experience Program, the student agrees to do his or her best to represent both family and school in a manner accepted by society.

Prior to approval for the Work Experience Program, each student and his or her parent or guardian must sign the agreement. Failure to comply with any part of this agreement will be considered cause for removal from the Work Experience Program.

_____
Student

_____
Parent/Guardian

Figure 1-3

TEACHER/EMPLOYER CONTACT SHEET

Student's Name _____

Employer's Name _____ Date _____

Student Work Supervisor _____

Phone Number _____ Mileage _____

Results _____

_____

Employer's Name _____ Date _____

Student Work Supervisor _____

Phone Number _____ Mileage _____

Results _____

_____

Employer's Name _____ Date _____

Student Work Supervisor _____

Phone Number _____ Mileage _____

Results _____

_____

Figure 1-4

STUDENT WORKER EVALUATION SHEET

Student _____   School _____

Job Title _____

Please indicate your evaluation of this worker by placing a check mark in the proper column. Specific comments or suggestions may be made in the last column. Please return to the teacher/supervisor.

JOB PERFORMANCE	Excellent	Good	Poor	Comments
Punctuality				
Attendance				
Follows instructions				
Quality of work				
Judgment				
Ability to work with others				

ATTITUDE	Excellent	Good	Poor	Comments
Cooperation with company rules				
Ability to accept criticism				
Courtesy				
Interest in work				

PERSONAL APPEARANCE	Excellent	Good	Poor	Comments
Appropriate dress				
Cleanliness				
Neatness				

Date _____   Employer's Signature _____

10   SOLID CONCEPTS ON SEVEN AREAS OF TEACHING—COMMUNICATING DIRECTLY

When you enter the confines of today's classroom, you are faced with a myriad of challenges. You must develop a personal series of philosophies, policies, and strategies that will help you work, teach, and survive amid those challenges and thereby become an effective teacher.

The truth is that we must all adjust and adapt our discipline procedures to the teaching assignment as presented to us each year. Whether it is the same grade with different students or a wholly new teaching assignment, that adjustment is part of being a professional. Listed here are seven areas to consider.

PHILOSOPHY

We must all have a philosophy of why we are in the classroom in the first place. For each person, this is different to some degree. The one, overriding point about a philosophy is that it must have a practical application; otherwise you are likely to be stuck in a quagmire of idealism. With no realistic application of your philosophy, you will not last long.

Your procedures evolving from your philosophy must work for the learning and betterment of the students and for your own satisfaction. If either of these two variables is lacking, the profession of teaching will soon become drudgery.

RELATING

Students need to know where you are coming from in terms of relating to them and their interactions. A clear explanation of the following basic precepts of teacher-student relationships will help students understand why you react as you do.

➤ You are hired here as a teacher. This is your job. You are not here to socialize. You are not part of the student social environment. You are the paid educational leader of this group of young people. Because your roles are different, the students are not to treat you like the person at the next desk. While you will be friendly, you are not, nor can you become, pals or best friends with them.

➤ Inform students that in your dealings with them, your goal is to maximize their assimilation of knowledge through a positive learning environment. Tell students that they will run into problems with you if their behavior does anything to harm or destroy that positive learning environment for themselves or others. Your disciplinary actions are to be seen as an attempt to correct their behavior so the positive learning environment can be maintained.

23

- Students will always have the right to communicate with you. You will address each issue on its own merits and not carry grudges or baggage from any other year or from having had any of their siblings in a previous class. Your relationship with them will be pure, direct, and honest.

- In the event a major issue comes up that affects all, the students are to get the support of the whole class, and at that point you will work it out with them.

- Students must have an understanding of where their problems come from. You must make students realize that teachers are not the source of their problems. Some students have a generalized idea that teachers cause them their greatest amount of trouble. Tell students to examine the amount of anxiety or problems resulting from assignments or from interactions with teachers and to compare this with the degree of grief originating with their peers. The teacher-based problems will be insignificant when compared to how their "friends" treat them.

WORK

Schoolwork is mandatory for all students if they are to get an education. In special circumstances, that work must be modified to accommodate differing abilities, but all students must do their assigned work.

Teachers and others have been blamed over the years for lack of student success. It should be stressed to the students that the teacher is not responsible for a student's choosing failure instead of success. The student has clear choices to do or not to do a particular amount of work. The student will find failure if he or she chooses not to work and success if he or she chooses to work; it is basic and it is simple. This is the real world.

Certainly, a student who scores high on a test or other evaluation tool gives himself or herself the credit (I got an "A"). It therefore follows that if a student scores low, he or she must also take the responsibility and not say, "Ms. Jones gave me an F." Grades are earned through choices.

DISCIPLINE

It is crucial for students to know what your discipline policies are. They must be aware of how far you will allow yourself to be pushed or what your level of tolerance is.

Here is one perspective:

- The first offense or breach of your discipline program will result in a lecture from the teacher (apart from the rest of the students).

- The second offense will cause the student to spend time in the office until the teacher, counselor, or principal can talk with the student.

- The third offense will see the student's parent or guardian being asked to come in for a discussion of the matter and a resultant plan of action developed with contracts, deadlines, and so on.

- The fourth offense will cause the student to be suspended from school (if the school jurisdiction allows it). When this occurs, the student must understand that this final or fourth stage represents the need to provide for the positive learning environment of the other students. This student's actions have placed him or her outside that environment by his or her own free will.

TIME MANAGEMENT

Students are at school for one purpose—to fulfill their need to get an education. Learning time-space importance is an integral part of that education. Being late and having to return to their lockers for materials are major disruptions of the classroom procedures—and therefore the learning process—for themselves and others.

Students must arrive on time and have the necessary materials to work with. If a student must return to his or her locker for books, pens, or other materials, he or she is considered late for class by the teacher, and this should be reported to the school office. The same sanctions should apply to this student as to a student who comes to class late.

TALKING

When the teacher is talking, the students are not to talk. When a student is talking on a point in the class, no other student is to cause interference by talking. A basic, fundamental rule of life applies here. There are times when it is best to use your discretion and keep your mouth shut.

RULES

Students love rules. It gives them a feeling of security as they have a clearly defined set of parameters. Students also love rules for another reason. They love to break them. Every rule made by you in the classroom is open to be broken down somehow by the students. This causes rules to become vague, weak, or meaningless at times. In the hustle and bustle of the classroom, combined with the differences among students, the application of rules can become fuzzy because all rules

- ➡ can be broadened
- ➡ can be eliminated
- ➡ can be adapted to a situation
- ➡ can be unfair (a fair rule is the Nirvana of teaching)
- ➡ can be forgotten

To avoid the erosion of classroom and school rules, keep a vigilant eye on how you react to the students and therefore add to the weathering process.

To maintain the validity of rules:

- ➡ Rules should be consistent, agreed upon, and adhered to by all staff members. This is important in terms of modeling—especially for students from dysfunctional or nonexistent families.

- ➡ Watch how much leeway you allow when applying the rules. The more leeway, the more likely the rules will become of less value.

- ➡ Apply rules equally for boys and for girls.

- ➡ Base your rules around a central working theme, such as "Students in our school will have respect for self, others, and the property of the school and its students." With a central strong theme, you have a frame of reference from which to develop rules that will be difficult to erode.

- ➡ Forgive yourself when problems arise from rules you have established.

GUIDELINES FOR A PROBLEM-FREE MUSEUM OR ART GALLERY FIELD TRIP

Teachers are very good at taking students on field trips, educational outings of all sorts, and tours of various facilities when they are available. These outings or field trips serve to enhance or reinforce the material learned in the regular classroom.

Two of the most common places or locations teachers take students are art galleries and museums—some of the most enriching environments to bring students to because of the quantity and quality of items for students to see and consider. Indeed, whole classrooms of students have been flown to Washington, D.C., to tour the Smithsonian. It is difficult to find a more valuable educational complex.

To avoid the problems that can be associated with a museum or art gallery field trip, the following ten guidelines will help you have a smooth and trouble-free visit to a museum or art gallery.

1. Go to the gallery or museum ahead of time to check out the viability of the field trip and to familiarize yourself with the surroundings.

2. Notify the museum or gallery authorities that you are planning a field trip to their location. Obtain the needed brochures or pamphlets. Ask if they have tours with guides for your age of student.

3. If it is possible, take your students to museums that have hands-on or interactive highlights. Students love to touch, handle, or manipulate widgets and gadgets. These add to the quality of the field trip.

4. Check out security procedures of the museum or gallery. Some galleries, for example, will send a security guard to follow the students as they tour the building to ensure that students do not touch the priceless Renoir.

5. Prepare an orientation package that will give students things to look for, write about, or check off. This package must be as comprehensive as possible.
   If left on their own without a work package at a museum, for example, they are likely to run through the display areas and emerge on the other side saying, "It was just a bunch of old stuff!"

6. Send students in age-appropriate groups. Most museum and art galleries have specific tours geared to differing age levels.

7. Explain the restrictions and the need for those restrictions to the students prior to starting the field trip.

8. The younger the students, the greater the need for chaperons.

9. Take a cellular phone with you on all field trips.

10. Tell the students of a location in or near the museum or gallery to go to if they should get lost.

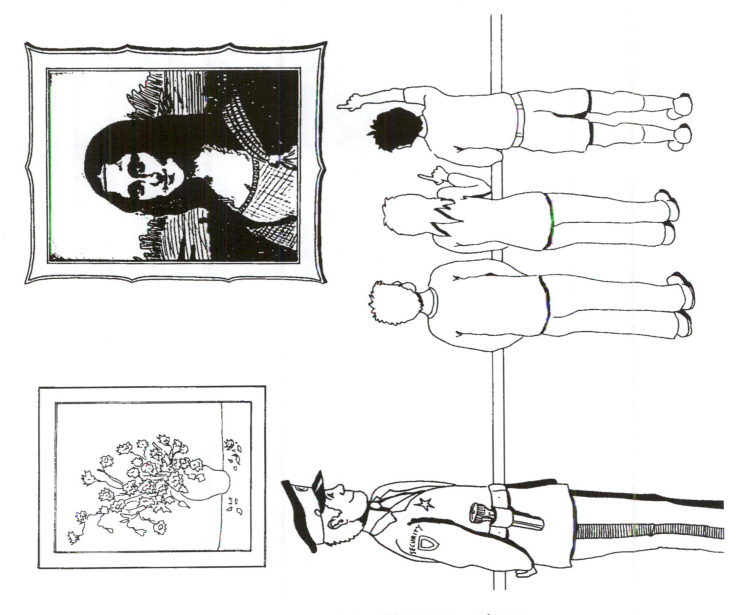

12 SOLVING PROBLEMS FOR THE DO-NOTHING, UNMOTIVATED, APATHETIC STUDENT

Many students do not seem to have a sense of motivation toward school work. The reasons these students do not have any personal drive or ambition are as many and varied as there are individuals with the problem.

Long thought of as a problem of the lower socioeconomic level student, this is now known not to be the case. Apathetic, do-nothing students can come from any status in society.

The following three general categories of students refuse to, or cannot, do the work required at school.

1. The emotionally poor student. He or she may be from a family that gave him or her all the material goodies of the culture but none of the real love that counts. His or her self-talk includes statements like "Why should I do school—work; nobody cares."

2. The economically and socially disadvantaged. The world he or she is from is often not able to promote academic success. Performance in school is not seen as a positive event within the child's sphere of influence.

3. The student who falls between the cracks. He or she is not low enough in skills to qualify for special and remedial programs but is not academically talented enough to keep up with the mainstream.

The apathetic or unmotivated student has the potential to become a behavior problem. The trick here is to identify and tap into this student's needs. Each case is unique, and professional discretion in decision making is essential. Flexibility is the key. With this student, hard and rigid expectations for performance will only hurt you.

SOME CONCEPTS THAT CAN HELP

1. Make doubly sure the work the student is asked to do is not beyond his or her skill level. Many students will adopt the apathetic, do-nothing guise because they are afraid to fail.

28

2. Many of these students do not have a well-developed sense of altruism; they have accomplished little in their lives to promote the care and well-being of others less fortunate than themselves. As a result, they can be very self-centered and have little grasp of the real world. It therefore may be helpful to such a student to participate in a school volunteer program (if you think the personality of the student is suitable). In a volunteer program, the student is exposed to people with greater needs than his or her own. The student could be placed in a Candy Stripe program at a local hospital or as a teacher assistant for children with severe physical or emotional handicaps. This dose of reality will sometimes jog the apathetic student into appreciating the skills he or she has.

3. If the problem with the apathetic student lies in getting immediate assignments completed in class, tell the student to bring his or her notebook to your desk. You write down in the notebook the numbers of the questions that you want completed. Leave enough blank space for answers. Tell the student you want to see every blank space filled with work by the end of the period. This is a workable frame of reference for the student, and often the task will be completed because you gave him or her an attainable, short-term goal.

4. Sometimes, apathetic students think they do not have to work because they are athletically inclined and are specializing in a particular sport. These students may feel that they are going to make it to the "pros," so why should they work in school; they are going to make "big bucks" in the big leagues.

   With this type of student, parent contact is very important. The parents most likely have been supporting their children in the sports arena, and so it follows that these parents usually will be cooperative. With good back-and-forth-communication, these students will get away with very little.

   As a last resort, contact a student's coach and try to enlist him or her as an ally because you are both working for the benefit of "The World's Greatest Athlete."

   One word of caution: The coach or the sports establishment may be part of the problem. Some teams have been known to arrive home from games after midnight or at three or four in the morning during the school week. What you end up with at school time is a totally exhausted student. The apathy or lack of motivation is nothing more than the performing ability of one "tuckered out" kid.

   One final variable to watch for in the student who lives and breathes to "make the pros": When the reality hits home that he or she did not make the farm team for the NHL or the NBA, that student may take a turn for the apathetic worst. If you note any distinct change in behavior, contact a parent to discuss the problem.

5. Hone your positive reinforcement skills; show the student that you care. Continuously reinforce and reward this student with a special performance program wherein the student works to earn tokens that are used to buy privileges. A note here: The reward system should be user-friendly for you, such as a marble dropped into a jar for every day of good work. When the jar gets full or up to a certain amount, the student gets a reward. Some behavior modification ideas will work but require a lot of record keeping and teacher downtime. Use the KIS-E principle: Keep it simple—and effective.

6. Help the apathetic student to set goals and then attain them. First, do the assignments in a section, then proceed to assignments in a chapter, and so on, until larger goals are within reach. Breaking down the largest goal (pass the class or year) into small, more foreseeable goals or sections allows room for success, which in turn will bring up a student's overall self-esteem.

13

UNDERSTANDING PEER INFLUENCES

Studies have shown that very few teenagers will change their peer group structure or peer group itself when counseled to do so. Because of immaturity in social understanding, combined with an undeveloped ability to predict the net result of their own behaviors or the behavior of their peers, students will often cling to peer relationships even after abuse. They are unable to see the *comparison level of alternatives*, that point where forming new relationships is more worthwhile than maintaining the ones they have now.

Peer group membership, especially among girls, tends to be rigid and exclusive. It therefore becomes difficult to break into a new group, although it can be done. Male peer groups tend to be slightly more flexible in terms of group membership, so peer group changes occur more often.

One perplexing phenomenon applies to teachers and parents in their effort to help students see how poor-quality friends will affect them. That is, the more you tell a student or child that a friend is a negative influence, the more tightly the student is drawn to that negative peer. The child rationalizes the fears of the parents or teacher/counselor by saying something like "Johnny or Judy is not that bad" or "He or she did drugs only a few times; he or she won't get me involved." The student or child you are trying to help will create a series of arguments with which to counter your concerns about the negative peers or friends. This series of rationalizations will still be used by the teenager when the negative friend or peer is in obvious trouble (arrested, drug overdose, etc.)

This is the problem. What can you do about it?

1. Avoid a confrontation; rather, a good solid discussion of what to watch for—without naming names—will educate the student to recognize the problems coming from his or her peers.

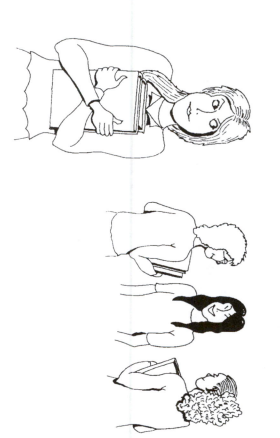

30

2. Peer and antidrug education programs should begin at the primary level. By instilling the proper values early, you can avoid some of the problems.

3. Develop a positive peer helper program from the many available. In this type of arrangement, students help students. The peers need some training by the teacher or counselor in the necessary social skills to be effective as peer helpers. Students will listen to a peer helper if that peer or student is a significant other. Therefore, careful selection of peer counselors is essential; credibility is important. It is also necessary to have a variety of personality types as your peer counselors. Not all students will relate to the same type of person.

4. Some teachers will connect with certain students. It may be possible to use this when dealing with negative peers. A right word or properly timed statement might make the student aware of the trouble his or her peers will cause him or her.

5. Create the "counselor of the open door" program. With this, students are free to walk into the counselor's office, when he or she is not busy, to discuss peer and other problems. Much will come out of these sessions to help students adjust to the violent and abusive nature of their friends.

6. There are a number of anti-violence, anti-abuse awareness programs now available. These programs tell students what abuse is, what to watch for, and how to protect themselves. They can be taught to the whole classroom at one time. These programs seek to prevent violence among peers as well as family members.

Many young people will support their friends even to the point of fighting with their parents. This is because the student feels that her or his parents will always be there, but their friends may abandon them. The peers must, therefore, be appeased to be maintained. This appeasement results only in sporadic reinforcement from their friends. It is this sporadic reinforcement that is most effective in perpetuating the need for more appeasement and, therefore, adherence to the peer group.

14

IT'S A SEEDY THING TO DO

In all of education, one behavior pattern irks teachers above all else. This pattern is annoying to anyone having the misfortune of being nearby when a student does this. I am referring to the spitting out of sunflower seed shells. The process of eating sunflower seeds in itself is not the problem; it is the disposal of the shells or husks of this product.

When students chew these seeds in class, they have little care or concern for the environment of their fellow students or the students who will come to that classroom after them. Quite often, the chewing student will just spit the husks on the floor, but others are more discreet and will drop the husks on the floor as the bell rings, ending the class. In the hustle and bustle of student movement, you are unlikely to catch the offender before he or she has entered another class in a different part of the school. This creates further problems because you have to chase after the errant student to bring him or her back to clean up—and it is further complicated by what you are doing with the new class you have in your room. If your new students are writing a test, for example, you will not want that new group to be disturbed by a student cleaning up.

Sunflower seeds are an annoyance, no matter how you look at it. Your best defense against this problem is to have a strongly enforced policy against this product and put up the "This Is a NO Sunflower Seed Zone" poster (Figure 1-5) in several prominent locations around your school.

Figure 1-5

This Is a NO Sunflower Seed Zone

33

HOW TO DEAL WITH THE DISCIPLINE PROBLEMS OF BRIGHT, HIGH-PERFORMANCE STUDENTS AND THE PARENTS OF THOSE STUDENTS

Teachers and administrators are always concerned about the behavior problems at the low end of the academic scale. There is, however, another group that can create an even greater problem in the classroom in terms of behavior and performance—not only for the teacher but for the remainder of the class as well. This is the bright, high-performance student whose goal is the year-end school awards and who has a "win-at-all-costs" attitude for his or her own aggrandizement.

The parents of these children usually fall into one of three general categories. These are:

1. The normal, average parent who is supportive and not overly critical. Most of the bright students' parents are in this group.

2. The parent who has a fear of his or her child and is dominated by him or her.

3. The equally high performance, highly critical parent who follows every step his or her child makes at school or elsewhere. This parent sees his or her child as number one and wants to keep it that way.

It is very difficult for most parents to be truly objective about their own children. With parents from group 3, you have the potential for problems in the normal ongoings of the classroom because you must provide programs for such a child, but you cannot favor that child over any other.

SOME USEFUL GUIDELINES

1. Develop enrichment programs to keep this student on task. A common complaint of this child—echoed by the parents—is that the child is bored with the regular curriculum, which is geared to the average student. The "boredom" excuse has been used unfairly against teachers when this bright, aggressive child becomes a behavior problem for other reasons. Be aware of this. Bright, high-performance students are human, too, and can be a source of problems because of personality conflicts, trouble at home, or the bravado of youth.

2. Watch how many extra percentage points you give to this student. At the end of the year, you could be faced with a student having 105 percent in a subject and a computer report card program that will not handle it. In one case, a student came close to suing the school to ensure that his report card read 112 percent in math. This also caused no end of grief when it came to school award time.

3. Dot your *i*'s and cross your *t*'s with this type of student. This applies to the following areas:

➡ Marks and grade scores.

➡ Problem and behavior record keeping.

➡ Awards criteria and qualifications. They must be rigid, exact, and impartial. If you are not perfectly clear in any aspect of this, you will be called on it. It is important that the awards criteria be set at the beginning of the school year and not be tailored or modified during the year.

4. Do not appear to favor the bright, aggressive student because he or she is reliable. Search for answers, errand runners, and workers from all the students in the class equally. Develop some kind of draw system for this.

5. The bright, aggressive student is often from an upper middle class, highly educated family. This can be a source of extra problems for you in the classroom if and when you have a dispute with that child. A small percentage of this group will not adhere to due process to resolve problems. That due process should begin by contacting the teacher and principal who deal directly with the student. Those parents may go straight to the director or superintendent of education of the school board and lodge their complaint there. These people frequently feel that they are beyond the teacher and principal and will deal only with those in top authority.

It is best to discourage this because directors and superintendents are busy people; they will recognize it as a classroom- or school-based problem and react accordingly. It is wise, therefore, in an early school newsletter to parents to describe the due-process procedures for resolving a classroom or school dispute. The thrust of that message should be to contact the teacher or principal first in the event of a dispute or other problem at the school involving their child. This should be a clearly stated open policy that directors and superintendents of education can fall back on.

6. Be prepared for a continuous barrage of questions from this type of student. Most are very inquisitive and will want definitive answers. This is great; however, you must teach proper protocol in this. They are not to interrupt when you are talking to others or presenting a lesson, nor are they to interfere when you are trying to solve a problem for someone else. Strict guidelines must be created and adhered to in these areas.

35

16

GUIDELINES FOR DEALING WITH SEXUAL HARASSMENT ANYWHERE IN THE SCHOOL ENVIRONMENT

Sexual harassment has been a problem for men and women over time as they have worked and associated together. We are sexual beings and this is not always expressed appropriately.

The amount of sexual harassment is not any greater in today's society than it has been at any other time; however, the recognition of this very real problem has increased through the diligence of various rights advocacy groups throughout the nation. People on the job are no longer as willing to tolerate this form of abuse in their place of employment—in schools or any other work location. This awareness is a good thing getting better. In no way should a person have to endure the unwanted sexual fantasies or advances of any other person.

For a better understanding of the problem, a working definition of what sexual harassment is follows: "Sexual harassment occurs when people cause unwanted discomfort, anxiety, embarrassment, degradation, or debasement of another individual, either overtly or subtly and covertly through sexual means or references."

One of the reasons this problem continues to exist is that the victim will often not report the incident to the authorities because he or she may consider it too trivial or be fearful of retaliation from a work superior. The victim may fear a generalized reprisal coming from the community he or she lives in. If you do not take action on the incident, there is a strong likelihood the problem will recur—only worse. Here are some guidelines to help you deal with sexual harassment while at school.

A. *Recognition:*

1. Sexist jokes—verbally or in printed form, like a cartoon or written jokes on the bulletin board.

2. Continuous advances for sexual favors, especially after refusal.

3. Nonaccidental violation of your personal body space.

4. Nonaccidental touching of your body.

5. Sexual innuendos, no matter how subtly stated.

B. *What You Can Do When It Happens:*

1. Contact a trusted colleague for advice and support.

2. Nip the problem in the bud. Say to the person or write on the cartoons, "This is sexual harassment." This quick recognition will often deter any further problems.

3. Contact your teachers' association for advice and support.

4. Contact a sexual harassment support group in your area or community.

5. Contact your local council for human rights group.

6. Be prepared for any action. Record times, dates, locations, and the context of the harassment.

7. Dress modestly.

8. Men must report incidents of sexual harassment much more than they do.

9. Seek legal counsel. A complete knowledge of your rights will protect you.

10. Experience has shown that it is not a good idea to subject the victim of sexual harassment to a process of mediation. The increased trauma to the victim as he or she faces the harasser doubles the pain from the incident.

17

THE FIVE-STEP PROBLEM SOLVER

In the ongoing dynamics of student relationships in schools, there are often conflicts and individually created problems. Many of these conflicts and problems can escalate into larger confrontations involving parents—and even legal action. It is best to head off the problems or disputes before they get a chance to blossom into full-blown calamities.

The two basic causes of interpersonal and other problems are selfishness by one of the parties to the dispute or a lack of communication by someone. The Five-Step Problem Solver Form (Figure 1-6) can be used with students to break down these two basic causes of problems. The form has been designed to be used when you have a conflict or dispute between two students, when you have a disruptive, behavior-problem student in the class, or when you have a student who has caused physical or other damage in the school.

The questions asked in the Five-Step Problem Solver Form target selfishness. This is accomplished in questions 1, 2, and 3, by asking the student to describe the situation and explain why he or she "chose" this behavior. The student is also asked to consider the effect that behavior had on others. These questions will not only expose motives but, when answered, cause the student to reveal "ownership" of his or own errant behavior.

RESOLUTION

PROBLEM

Question 4 is a future-directing question. The student is asked to predict the consequence if his or her behavior does not change and he or she continues to act in this poor way. Question 5 leads to resolution or to a mutually agreeable solution.

The form itself helps break down the second cause of problems; it promotes strong communication in the areas needed to resolve the dispute. It is concrete—the conflict written down in black and white. Understanding often occurs in the process of writing out the Five-Step Problem Solver Form.

How to Implement the Five-Step Problem Solver

1. Once you are informed of the dispute, you must separate the combatants or isolate the individual causing the problem and immediately give them the Five-Step Problem Solver Form to fill out. Usually, tempers will settle while the form is being filled out.

2. Once the student(s) has completed the form, teacher or supervisor must read the data. If there is only one student involved, then discussion of resolution can begin at this point.

   If, however, there are two or more students involved, each of the parties is to read (without interruptions) what he or she has written so all can hear. Remember, the teacher/supervisor must be present at all times when the parties are brought back together.

3. Once each student has heard the other's point of view, the teacher/supervisor is to initiate discussion between the students with a focus on the solution side of the problem—not the conflict side.

4. Students need this structured process to solve problems because, for the most part, they do not have mature social-problem-solving skills. The Five-Step Problem Solver helps the student break away from the unpredictability of cause-and-effect action and focus more on logical, mature deductive reasoning. In this way, you can turn a dispute into a safe learning experience for the child.

Two added features:

⬆ Students will often write down what they feel, but would not normally express those same sentiments when speaking.

⬆ If stories should change by the time the student gets home, and you are on the receiving end of a phone call from an angry parent, you now have a signed written record to show the parent. In fact, a student who has completed the Five-Step Problem Solver Form is much less likely to change the story by the time he or she gets home.

39

Figure 1-6

THE FIVE-STEP PROBLEM SOLVER FORM

1. Describe the nature of the situation or problem.

   _____

   _____

2. Why did you choose this behavior?

   _____

   _____

3. How did your behavior affect others?

   _____

   _____

4. What will happen if you continue to act this way?

   _____

   _____

5. Let's solve this problem. What can we do to reach a solution we can all live with?

   _____

   _____

Student Signature _____   Teacher/Supervisor Signature _____

MIKE'S STORY

It is not my intention in this work to speak personally on how I dealt or worked with this or that individual student; however, I feel that describing my personal experience with Mike will best tell you how to work with a student who—while not aggressively belligerent—has a chip on his or her shoulder.

Mike had developed a sense of personal bitterness toward life. That bitterness had been instilled in Mike through years of living in a dysfunctional family, poor school grades, and a need to be "street wise" in order to survive. Mike, it seemed, trudged through life with a feeling that nobody cared.

I was making my way around the classroom one day during English class when I saw that he looked askance at me. He was not working on the grammar assignment I had given him, but rather he was drawing a nature picture of some quality. As he stared at me, he had that look in his eye that he feared I was going to reprimand him for being off task, but I surprised him. I said, "Hey, Mike, what a great picture. Will you do a larger one like this for me to display on the bulletin board?" Mike's face lit up like the fireworks four days into July.

I got a large sheet of plain white paper for Mike to create my nature picture. Now, Mike was somewhat of a behavior problem in the other classes prior to this, but while creating the artwork for me, he was completely on task in the other classes to finish—so he could have extra time to work on the art project. I had made arrangements with my colleagues to facilitate this.

Everyone noticed a change in Mike. The simple act of keying into what was an important self-respect builder was of immeasurable value. Mike was a good artist, and I made use of this. He was not reprimanded for being off task in English, but instead, I reinforced him in an area that gave him much-needed self-esteem points.

The nature picture has been up on my bulletin board for three months now, and Mike will often see two or three students standing before it discussing the merits of the work. This has had a long-term effect on Mike. Other teachers tell me the positive change in Mike's attitude has prevailed to this day.

The Mikes of the school system are not hard to find. If you and I are able to tap into the things, events, processes, and circumstances that are important to this type of student in order to show him or her that we indeed do care, then his or her life and ours will be just that much better.

19

GUIDELINES FOR DEALING WITH
THE SCHOOL BULLY

The school bully has been a problem in one form or another since Adam and Eve's first child. The solution to the bully problem has never been an easy one because it concerns the interactive processes of people. Schools and school systems are in a double bind in the case of the school bully. The teachers and administrators must teach and, at the same time, protect the children in their charge. The person with the bullying tendencies must be taught and protected as well, even if he or she is intimidating others. The human rights of the bully must be totally protected in spite of the fact that he or she abrogates the rights of others.

If left unchecked, the school bully will inhibit the learning capacity of fellow students by mounting a campaign of manipulation through fear. That fear can be a strong inhibitor of action for a less physically or emotionally capable pupil. The bully's victim will be afraid to tell school officials and parents about the problem. How do you curtail the actions of the bullies at school in order to create a positive learning environment for everyone?

The following set of guidelines will allow educators to identify and alleviate the direct and indirect problems caused by the student with bullying behavior.

A. *Identification is the initial major concern. Here is a set of cues and behaviors to watch for:*

1. Watch for students who get reinforcement from their peers for negative actions.

2. Watch for the physically large and cocky student from a known socially dysfunctional background.

3. The school bully is rarely defined as that, but he or she will be known as having a number of behaviors already identified that need attention.

4. Watch for a gang or minigang led by an aggressive, boisterous student.

5. Watch for acts of intentional shoving and hitting that go beyond the normal student roughhousing.

6. Keep an eye out for socially deviant behaviors, such as spitting, threats, and intimidation.

B. *What the school can do:*

1. Create a Parent Alert newsletter. You should stress in this communication that you and the school authorities will take action if a child is bullied either at school or going to and from school. This is necessary because many parents have had these problems in the past and felt nothing was done about it. If parents know you will do everything in your power to defend their children, your home and school relations will be positive and strong.

2. Have a "problem" or "suggestion" box in the school office, so students can anonymously voice their concerns.

3. Because the bully thrives on reinforcement from peers and a semblance of power in seeing others fear him or her, the school should remove the identified bully from his or her peer group. This can be accomplished by having the student not arrive at school until five minutes after the morning bell has rung and not releasing this student until five minutes after the end-of-school bell has sounded. Recesses and noon hours are to be spent under supervision in the school office or in a classroom.

4. Do not have recess in your school (grade 5 and above). Have five-minute breaks between classes, thus cutting down the time available for this problem to occur.

5. Keep all students in a supervised lunchroom for the duration of the noon hour.

6. Place the bullying student in a work experience program within the school system (at another school, under the supervision and training of the custodial staff). This will give the student positive reinforcement for positive actions.

7. Have weekly rap sessions of twenty minutes with the student and the school authorities or counselor. This should be a problem-solution conference.

8. Stagger recesses if you have a problem of older students' bullying younger children.

9. Put the school rules of behavior on a bulletin board in the school. These rules must be read by every teacher to each classroom at least once a month. Inappropriate behaviors must be defined, so that the students have a clear idea of what is acceptable and what is not.

10. Be careful you do not fall into the self-fulfilling prophecy trap; that is, if a student exhibits bully-like behavior one year, it does not follow that he or she will have these same tendencies the following year. Judge each child on his or her own merits every year.

11. You can use tools like contracts and agreements to help change the behavior of the bully, but remember, no behavior modification program will work if there is not strong commitment. That commitment is built up by your being reliable, consistent, and fair in your reward systems.

44

20

DESK DISCIPLINE

You are the teacher of a grade 6 class that does not travel from room to room. In the normal circumstances of the day, you spot Clifford's desk. It looks like the Florida Coast during and after a hurricane. You know that Clifford is the most disorganized, messy, yet wonderful student you have ever met. How can you help the Cliffords of this world have some discipline over their desks?

A unique way to solve this problem is to give the student with the messy desk the "Your Desk Is a Disaster" note (Figure 1-7). This note informs the student in a pleasant, yet effective, way that his or her desk is in dire need of cleaning and reorganization.

The note has a space for you to write a specific deadline as to when the desk must be cleaned and organized for inspection. It works because it is a concrete and constant reminder of what must be accomplished and when.

Figure 1-7

Student _____

YOUR DESK IS A DISASTER

You will clean and organize
your desk by: _____
time & date

It will be inspected by: _____
teacher / supervisor

21 GUIDELINES FOR DEALING WITH VANDALISM

Many schools are the victims of vandalism. This becomes a multifold problem because schools have precious few resources to spend on materials and labor repair costs. Effective methods are needed, therefore, to prevent vandalism from happening in the first place. Just what can you do to prevent this age-old problem from occurring?

Use the following guidelines as they apply to you:

1. The key to any antivandalism program is accountability. Make the student, not the parents, pay for willful damage. Students must be made to work off costs at minimum wage. Failure to do so should result in formal charges by the police.

2. Have an ongoing reward system for best-looking or tidiest classroom, locker, desk, and so forth.

3. Make the people who write on or mar desks stay after school to expend some elbow grease cleaning all the desks in the classroom.

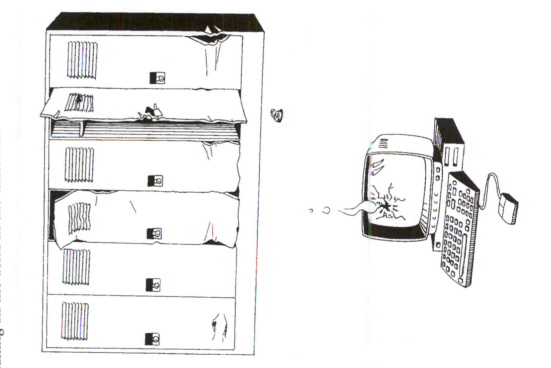

4. Develop a high-profile antivandalism policy with a list of improper behaviors and their consequences. Place this on a poster in the hall of the school. Vandalism occurs when people think there will be no consequences for their actions. Strong, effective, and meaningful penalties for this behavior must be in place.

5. Have a custodial guard system that regularly patrols the school areas.

6. Have a school thrust in the opposite direction; develop a beautification program (with the help of a service club). Bring in plants for the halls, plant trees, and use student art to decorate the foyer. Check your state, federal, and local governments for free help in this area.

7. Erase all examples of vandalism as soon as possible. It is not good to let destruction become visible, because destruction of school property will become the matter-of-fact, accepted thing to do.

8. Keep a gum scraper (paint scraper) in your desk. Refer to it often and give the students a demonstration. Tell them this is what they will have to do if they put gum under their desks or on the floor.

9. When a student is caught writing or carving on a desk or engaging in any other form of vandalism, have the student write out a note describing what was done. Either call in the parent or guardian for an interview or mail the note home to the student's family.

10. Develop the "Adopt a Wall" program (similar to the "Adopt a Highway" idea), in which a wall of the school is owned by a group of students. A little bureaucracy can be developed around this idea; students form a committee and hold meetings to make decisions about posters, decorations, and so on. Prizes and awards can be given for best displays. This creates ownership by the students of the school property.

11. Discipline policies with regard to school rules should have consistency. If students see that Mr. Smith does not do anything about writing on desks, they are sure to try it in Ms. Jackson's class. A staff meeting should be held to discuss consistency.

12. Have a school cleanup week where *everyone* participates. Watch for pockets or groups of students who think this environmentally friendly act is beneath their dignity. Do not let anyone use a stick with a nail in the end to pick up papers, chip bags, and other trash.

13. With the help of your local police, create a "tips" phone hot line for such crimes, because many acts of vandalism cannot be readily seen. Hacking a computer system is an example. Thousands of dollars worth of data can be rendered useless, and it may not be noticed for some time. Like most crimes of this sort, it will be bragged about sooner or later. If people can phone a tips line anonymously, they are more likely to inform you of this form of vandalism.

14. Bring in a guest speaker to talk about vandalism. The local police may be able to supply or tell you of an excellent speaker in this area.

15. Sometimes the student who causes vandalism is a person lacking skills in the area of socially acceptable behavior. If the student can be identified early enough, he or she should be given life skills training from one of the many excellent programs available.

There is no question that vandalism is a form of violence. It therefore is your right and duty to do all you can to protect students and school property.

48

VERBAL ABUSE GUIDELINES

Many teachers are attacked verbally by students. This form of abuse, coming from the student to the teacher, may have its cause in any one of a number of factors; it is usually not caused by any actions on the part of the teacher.

The problems of neglect, child abuse, and disintegrating families are not far from teachers. Many times, students will verbally vent their frustration if a small event triggers its release in the classroom or school.

When you are attacked verbally, you instantly have strong emotions about the situation, whether you precipitated it or not. To help you deal with a verbal attack directed at you, read the following set of guidelines for dealing with verbal abuse.

1. Keep your composure. You are the professional. Do not buy into the content of what the student is yelling.

2. Enlist the aid of another staff member, if possible.

3. If you feel yourself losing it, repeat in your mind the word "CALM." Spell it out in your mind.

4. Wait for the student to vent his or her feelings and catch a breath before you begin to speak.

5. If possible, remove the student from his or her own peers (audience).

49

6. Place the student in a timeout station in the class or at the school office if supervision and witnesses are in place.

7. Do not physically touch the student.

8. Do not yell at the student.

9. Look the student directly in the eye, set the boundaries of behavior, and tell the student what choices she or he has. Speak calmly but firmly.

10. Do not appear to cower or back down, thus reacting negatively and reinforcing the student's intimidation tactics.

11. If the verbal abuse continues to escalate, be prepared for the student to become physical; protect yourself by backing away and calling for assistance.

12. Document the totality of the incident as soon as possible. It is especially important to document any threats, statements about suicide, and other factors causing the problem.

13. Once a student has regained his or her sense of reasonableness, have the student write down on a plain sheet of paper what the problem was. This will have a further calming effect on the student and will possibly reveal more important details that you can use to help the student.

14. Remember that for most incidents of verbal abuse, to you from a student or from one student to another, the underlying factors will more than likely have nothing to do with the school.

15. Above all, you must remember that the rights and dignity of the student—and your rights—must be maintained at all times.

16. Once you are away from the situation, you must calm down. *If possible*, ask another teacher to cover your class for fifteen or twenty minutes while your blood pressure goes back to some semblance of normality.

23 THE ATTENDANCE CONCENTRATION IDEA

Teachers must take attendance at least once a day. Most teachers perform this task four to eight times a day, depending on the jurisdiction and the school circumstance.

When students are responding to their names, they often blankly reply "here" or "present." Some may appear half asleep, while others consider this a time to chat with friends. How can you make attendance taking into a "teachable moment" requiring a degree of concentration and alertness?

Use the following strategy to maximize concentration of your students at attendance-taking time. Tell them that they are not to say "present" or "here," but are to reply with a name or event from a previous day's lesson. For example, if you are studying Presidents of the United States, an appropriate response when a student's name is read out would be "Woodrow Wilson." When the next student's name is called, that person would respond with "Teddy Roosevelt," and so on. As long as there are enough presidents for each student to have a different response, there should be no repeating of president's names.

This idea strongly reinforces the learning of the previous day's or lesson's data. The students will have to be on their toes to come up with fresh responses; concentration is maintained during attendance taking, and you have achieved your "teachable moment."

If the previous days or lessons do not lend themselves to this idea, you may have the students respond with their favorite color or movie star.

51

24

TWO WAYS TO RESOLVE A MINOR STUDENT DISPUTE

In any social circumstance, like a school classroom, you will have a plethora of personalities, points of view, value systems, and differences in material ownership and respect. This can, and often does, lead to disputes. While these disputes (e.g., over a pencil case) may not be large at first, they can escalate to include parents and school officials.

How can you resolve a dispute between four or fewer students, so that the outcome is fair and equitable to all parties concerned?

TECHNIQUE 1

When this type of common dispute arises, it is best not to get involved yourself at the beginning of the dispute, but rather take the two areas is a private corner of the classroom, where you can keep a constant eye on the students and the rest of the class at the same time. This can be done only if you know the dispute is minor and no arguing will ensue. The other area to take the students to is a supervised location, like a guidance counselor's office.

Once you have located the students away from earshot of the other students in the class, you tell the dispute group that they are to work out a "proper solution to the problem." As simplistic as this seems, it works extremely well. They know you are looking but are far enough away to allow them to make a mature decision.

After the problem has been resolved by the participants, you interview each member of the group to see what the decision was.

TECHNIQUE 2

Have the participants to the dispute write out the nature of the dispute from their point of view on the Dispute Sheet (Figure 1-8).

When students write down their feelings about a situation or problem, they tend to calm down and logically think through the situation. Once the participants have written down the problem, and you have read the data, gather the people together to work through the problem. In this case, you are the moderator of a panel discussion. As moderator, you lead the students to compromise and resolution.

Both of these methods of resolving a minor student dispute require a degree of open communication. This is the key to the resolution of any dispute—large or small.

Figure 1-8

DISPUTE SHEET

Name: _____ Date: _____

What is the nature of the situation? _____

_____

_____

_____

Who was involved in this and how was each person involved? _____

_____

_____

How do you think this situation can be resolved or fixed? _____

_____

_____

25

THE BEHAVIOR STATION PROGRAM

You are busy teaching a class, and in the process, one student is a constant behavior problem. You have repeatedly told the student to settle down but proper behavior is not forthcoming. How do you manage this disruptive student and teach the rest of the class at the same time?

The answer is to develop a Behavior Station program within your classroom. With this idea, there are three distinct levels of concern regarding the behavior of the student. These levels are indicated on the worksheets associated with each level. This concept indicates to the student that you have placed him or her in a process that will increase your level of concern as the student moves from one station to another.

You will need three desks in your classroom in order to facilitate this idea. Ideally, these would be two corner desks in the classroom and one separate desk area.

If the student consistently misbehaves, you immediately move that student to the corner desk farthest away from his or her peers. This is called behavior station 1. You then have this student fill out the Behavior Description Sheet (Figure 1-9) of concern level one. This sheet requires the student to tell on paper why he or she is acting in a certain way.

If the student continues to misbehave and disrupt the class, you then move the student to behavior station 2, which is a second corner in the classroom that is not near her or his peers or audience.

When the student is at station 2, you give the child the Behavior Knowledge Sheet (Figure 1-10) of concern level two. You also provide the student with a dictionary at this time. Listed on the Behavior Knowledge Sheet are a number of words that relate to what the student is doing. You then tell the student to look up and write down the definitions of the words or ideas. The definitions themselves will serve to heighten the awareness in the student about his or her situation, what he or she is doing, and how it affects others.

The third station is the one station that is actually kept for this purpose. While the other behavior stations were ordinary school desks in two different corners of the class, this third location is a separate timeout behavior station in your classroom. It must be located in such a way as to be continually monitored by you as you teach the other students. The student in behavior station 3 is then given the Behavior Results Sheet (Figure 1-11) of concern level three to fill in. This is the final sheet the student will fill in. This Behavior Results Sheet will give the student a realization of what will follow should he or she misbehave in this final setting.

You will find that, when you place students in this program within your class, they will not make it past the second station in 95 percent of the cases. Their behavior will improve. There is, however, that 5 percent of the time when a student's misbehavior will push you to the limits and force you to send the child to the principal and to contact the parents. You are armed now, however, with three documents that relate information on this child; two of the documents, the Behavior Description Sheet and The Behavior Results Sheet, will give you a good deal of data in order to describe the child's situation to any powers that be.

Good communication between the teacher dealing with the behavior problem and the principal or school office is best, so that the steps of the program can work effectively. Ideally, all teachers in the school should use the program. This allows for consistency from class to class.

The Behavior Station Program helps you and the student in seven distinct ways:

1. It takes care of a behavior problem with a minimum of interruption for you while you are teaching the class or helping other individuals.

2. It removes the disruptive student from his or her peers (audience), thus settling down the peers.

3. It keeps the student on task while you are helping others.

4. It changes the paradigm (point of view) of the student from one of fooling around to an awareness of his or her behavior.

5. It is benign, nonthreatening and nondemeaning to the student.

6. It helps develop predicting skills in the student.

7. It causes the student to have a knowledge of the consequences of poor behavior.

Figure 1-9

CONCERN LEVEL ONE
BEHAVIOR DESCRIPTION SHEET

Name: _____   Date: _____

Answer all questions as completely as possible.

1.   This is the way I am acting today. _____

_____

_____

2.   This is the reason I am acting this way. _____

_____

_____

3.   These are the people I am doing this behavior for. _____

_____

_____

4.   This is what will happen if I continue to act this way. _____

_____

_____

Figure 1-10

CONCERN LEVEL TWO
BEHAVIOR KNOWLEDGE SHEET

Name: _____ Date: _____

Write out the meaning of the following words from the dictionary.

BEHAVIOR _____

MISBEHAVIOR _____

DISTRACTION _____

CONSEQUENCE _____

ATTENTION _____

COMPLAINT _____

ASSIGNMENT _____

APOLOGIZE _____

CONDUCT _____

MISCONDUCT _____

Figure 1-11

CONCERN LEVEL THREE (FINAL)
BEHAVIOR RESULTS SHEET

Name: _____   Date: _____

This is what I will say to the teacher about how I behaved today.

_____

_____

This is what I will say to the principal.

_____

_____

This is what my parents will say when the principal contacts them.

_____

_____

26

SOLVING PROBLEMS BEFORE, DURING, AND AFTER THE SCHOOL DANCE

The school dance can be a pleasing and positive experience for the students. It allows for quality interaction if all goes well. Many schools, however, have moved away from any form of extracurricular activity, such as a school dance, for various and valid reasons. Many other schools still have dances for their students and see this as an important recreational activity with meaningful social consequences.

If the school dance is to function properly, there are several guidelines that should be adhered to. These are as follows:

1. The doors allowing students into the dance, especially at a junior high school level, should be open for only one-half hour. For example, the doors should be open from 7:30 to 8:00 P.M. No student should be admitted after 8:00 P.M. The only exception to this is if the supervising persons had received a phone call or a note from a parent *prior* to the dance, stating that, due to circumstances, the child will be late arriving.

2. Dance tickets sold to the students should not be interchangeable and must be purchased in advance. It is best to write the student's name on the dance ticket at the time of purchase.

3. Whether you want to operate a canteen is at your discretion. The canteen duties are best delegated to a school fund—raising project group who can work properly with the dance committee. Usually, the sale of environmentally friendly products at the canteen is a good idea.

59

4. The biggest problem at a school dance is how to prevent drugs or alcohol from entering the premises. Here are some ideas:

a. If students have lockers in or near the gym, they must be cleaned out and the locks removed prior to the dance.

b. There should be a coat-check outside the gym in a separate classroom. That coat-check classroom should not be at ground level where a window can be opened.

c. The gym doors and windows, as well as the windows in the gym washroom or shower areas, should not be available for the passage of liquor or drugs.

d. Check the washrooms before, during, and after the dance. Of course, the most important check is prior to the dance; especially check the toilet tanks.

e. Do not allow students to bring oranges to the dance and do not allow students who have eaten oranges (if you can determine this) into the dance area. One of the oldest tricks in the book is to inject vodka into oranges with a hypodermic needle and then eat the oranges while the event is on.

f. Have a one-way door policy for the dance. If students leave, they should not be allowed to reenter.

g. If your school board does not have a policy on how to handle students who come to your dance drunk or high, then your school should seek legal counsel before any dance is undertaken.

5. Insist that students sign in any guests at the school office prior to the dance. Students should be notified the day before the dance if a guest was not approved.

6. The number of chaperons, of course, must be relative to the group. If the required number of chaperons is not forthcoming from the parents of the students, then the dance should be cancelled. Worst-case scenarios can, do, and are more likely to happen if you are understaffed in the area of chaperons.

7. Gum should not be allowed at the school dance. Scraping gum off the gym floor is not normally an enjoyable postdance experience.

8. It is very important that students avoid walking home after the dance. This should be stressed to the students as part of the advertising for the dance, so they can make proper transportation arrangements. If walking home is unavoidable, suggest to the students that they do so in groups of not fewer than three.

9. Whether to allow for parent-only-run dances is at your discretion. If the dance is held outside your facility, you may still be held accountable for problems that occur at the dance if you allow the parents to advertise for the dance in your school.

10. If a parent-run dance is to be held in your school gym without teacher supervisors, it is best for your school board to develop a policy on this.

60

27

THE BEHAVIOR CONTROL TICKET

Some students just will not listen. You can tell them a thousand times to quiet down or to improve their behavior, but your words will fall on deaf ears. This type of student has learned over the years to tune out anyone who gives a behavior control command or advice. This student often needs something concrete in front of him or her to be a constant reminder of the need to reform his or her behavior.

One solid idea that will work is to use the Behavior Control Ticket (Figure 1-12). This ticket should be photocopied onto heavy or stiff paper.

When a student will not listen or is a behavior problem, you present the ticket to the student and tell him or her that the following list of rules now applies:

1. Students with the ticket will have no communication with others.

2. The student with the ticket is to move his or her desk to the corner of the room and face the wall.

3. The teacher's initials will be placed at the end of the student's work, so the teacher can see how much new work is accomplished on this day.

4. Permission request for anything (e.g., washroom) must be written out and presented to the teacher after properly putting the hand up in the normal fashion.

5. The student will immediately answer the questions on the behavior control ticket.

The Behavior Control Ticket works well because it serves as a concrete reminder of the problem, as it isolates the student from his or her peer group within the classroom. It has a built-in series of questions for the student to focus upon, thus directing the student to something useful.

It must be remembered, however, that tickets or programs like this are only as good as your consistency in implementing and enforcing the details.

Figure 1-12
BEHAVIOR CONTROL TICKETS

BEHAVIOR CONTROL

Paragraph Answers Required:

A. Describe in detail the reason(s) you received the behavior control ticket
  - Why did you choose this behavior?
  - Who else was involved and why?
  - What were the consequences or results of what you chose to do?
B. How do you think the other students feel when you act this way?
C. Describe the reasons teachers need the classroom to be a place to learn.
D. Describe how you plan to change things for the better.

BEHAVIOR CONTROL

Paragraph Answers Required:

A. Describe in detail the reason(s) you received the behavior control ticket
  - Why did you choose this behavior?
  - Who else was involved and why?
  - What were the consequences or results of what you chose to do?
B. How do you think the other students feel when you act this way?
C. Describe the reasons teachers need the classroom to be a place to learn.
D. Describe how you plan to change things for the better.

28

HALLWAY AND WASHROOM PROBLEM SOLVERS

Many of the behavior anomalies that occur at school do so in the hallways—supposedly away from the prying eyes of teachers and custodial staff. It therefore becomes necessary to monitor and maintain control of the hallways and washroom facilities.

The following set of guidelines and problem solvers will help you develop a working policy for your school in order to protect students and property in and around halls and washrooms.

1. Every school needs consistency and agreement among the teachers to maintain the same level of discipline throughout all the halls and washrooms of the school.

2. The hallway and washroom behavior policy should be explained to the students at a general assembly at the start of school.

3. No student should be seen wandering or loitering in the halls during class times. Use the reproducible sign included here as a constant reminder (Figure 1-13).

4. It may be advisable to replace or cover the breakable plasterboard walls with hardboard or plywood in strategic areas—stairwells, washrooms, and so forth.

5. Some kind of hallway monitoring system is needed for each break, recess, or noon hour.

6. Washrooms can be a hangout for toughs. Constant, regular supervision of this area is essential.

7. If the lockers are located in the hall, make sure you assign lockers so you can separate personalities.

8. Appoint hall monitors whose duties include picking up papers, reporting problems, and so on. This job should be assigned on a rotating basis.

9. Once in a while, ask this question of your students, "Are any of you having any trouble with people or other things in the hall or washroom?" The answers should be written and not verbal. Confidentiality is important.

Figure 1-13
HALL AND WASHROOM SIGN

HALL and WASHROOM

WANDERING

and

LOITERING

during class time

PROHIBITED

SEATING PLAN MANIPULATION

Children are very social beings and many dynamics of group activity occur at the school level that would not be seen or have the chance to develop elsewhere. As part of the process of any functioning classroom, friends are made and antagonisms are created. This interaction can interfere with the educational process.

One way of controlling the behavior of the group is to have a seating plan for everything. This means that you create a seating plan not only for those times when students are at their desks in front of you but also for those times when everyone is seated in the gym for a concert or on the grass outside doing "nature art."

This seating-plan-for-everything concept allows you to manipulate who sits where and thus control which personalities sit near one another. This, of course, helps reduce discipline problems. This idea can be extended to line-ups and other places where the group gathers and has the potential to get out of hand.

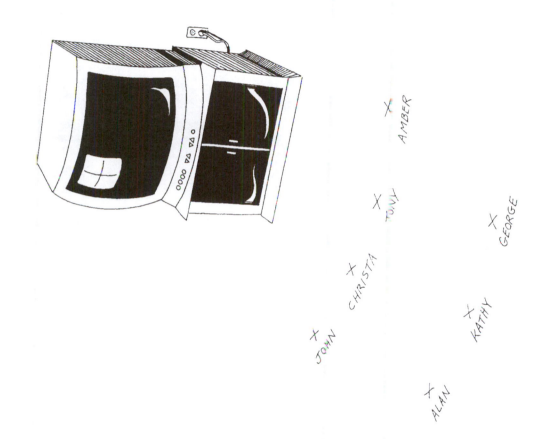

GUIDELINES FOR DEALING WITH STUDENTS WITH SHORT ATTENTION SPANS

The reasons some students are not able to concentrate are as varied and diverse as are the students in this situation—specific reasons, such as fetal alcohol syndrome (FAS) or lack of nourishment or sleep, as well as general reasons, stemming from all the problems inherent in a dysfunctional family.

The reasons may be many and varied, but that does not help you in the classroom. Your mandate is to educate this child to the best of your ability and the child's ability along with the twenty-seven or so other students who may have their own learning problems.

In teaching this short-attention-span student, some of your greatest challenges and greatest joys will come.

So what do you do? Here are some guidelines:

1. This student must be seen as a person of worth equal to that of any student in your classroom.

2. Place the short-attention-span student in a group of highly motivated, on-task students. When possible, make this student work in partnership with an aggressive, congenial mentor.

3. Make sure the classroom is never overheated. A temperature at exactly normal or one degree below normal will help prevent this person from getting drowsy.

4. Change topics three times in a period, for example, lecture, workbook assignment, then a video on the subject.

5. Create more physically interactive programs for this student. This is easy to say but not that easy to do; it may require the student to be in a totally or partially specialized program, if your school can afford it.

6. It is important to have a quality computer program for this type of student. The activities on the screen help to keep the student on task.

7. Work in learning kits that are instantly self-rewarding or have quick feedback. In other words, the learning kit should be designed to have the goals very close to the work being done.

8. The short-attention-span student would truly benefit from more use of manipulatives (blocks, etc.) when working in math or arithmetic.

9. Remember, having a short attention span does not necessarily mean the student lacks academic ability. Some very bright people can absorb fast and therefore have a low boredom tolerance. This may cause them not to concentrate very long on one area.

10. Short attention spans are often related to diet. It is possible that this student either is hungry or eats too much junk food. This can be improved by education.

66

EIGHTEEN WAYS TO PREVENT THEFT IN SCHOOL

In the modern classroom, you, the teacher, must deal with quite a few of the positives and negatives that society has to offer. It is necessary for you to do everything in your power to minimize the theft potential in your classroom. This applies to the rest of the school environment as well.

Here are eighteen ways to help prevent theft:

1. Lock your important files and personal valuables in a filing cabinet; an extra padlock is best. The mounting hardware is easily installed using two small u-bolts with threads on them.

2. Tell students to mark everything they own with either their names or student numbers.

3. Discourage students from bringing valuable portable radios, disk players, and other possessions to school.

4. When you or a student collects money for a school event, make a show of informing the students that you do not store the money in your classroom.

5. Do not bring your expensive CD, record, videotape, or audiotape collection to school.

6. Do not bring large sums of cash to school. If you must bring that $400.00 to pay your car repair bill after school, lock it up at the office.

7. Change the locks on your storage areas every four months—especially combination locks.

8. Make sure (even the best) students are not watching you when you unlock any combination lock.

9. Do not leave your school keys on your desk.

10. Promote the use of lockable lockers instead of desks for student storage.

11. Have a lock exchange policy, so students can turn in locks from their lockers when they suspect others have learned the combination.

12. Discourage the sharing of lockers, equipment, and clothing.

13. Tie daily used items to your desk—hole punch, pen, stapler, and so on.

14. Do not take valuable items, such as a watch, in exchange for the temporary use of a pen and do not store watches for students during gym times. You are accepting responsibility in this case. If the watch disappears, your troubles have just begun.

15. Do not wear your good leather jacket to school—or any other article of clothing that has a high pawn shop value.

16. Insist that the staff coat rack be out of sight in the staff room.

17. Make sure the school bike rack is in plain view from the office or a classroom.

18. Never take your purse to the classroom if you cannot lock it up.

Losing an item by theft is an intensely angering event. The feeling of initial helplessness about where to turn or what to do is agonizing, to say the least. This is one of those situations in life when an ounce of prevention is truly a treasured thing because the cure is often long, dragged out, and many times not forthcoming.

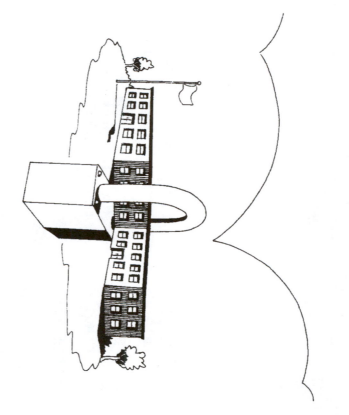

68

32

HELPING THE STUDENT WHO IS ALWAYS LATE

Many students do not have a relationship with the clock on the wall. To them, time is a vague, relative experience at best, and showing up late for class is not a goal to be attained. For others, showing up late for school is an attempt at juvenile rebellion. We all know this, so what do you do? Well, here are some ways you and I can help the tardy student:

1. Many students are continually late because of problems associated with a dysfunctional family. Often, these students have not had breakfast in the morning. It would help this type of student if the school had a breakfast program before school; it would get the students to school and eliminate some of the lethargy associated with improper diet.

2. At the high school level, the students have had several years' experience coming to school, so there should be no excuse for continuous late behavior. One idea that has a tremendous deterrent effect on students and causes them to make sure they arrive at class on time is to have them stop at the door if they are late and sing a song before they are allowed to enter the classroom. (Care should be taken not to embarrass any student.)

3. Some people in the community will volunteer to phone homes of the always late student in the morning. This encourages them to get started for the day.

4. Special programs can be developed that have a different paradigm regarding time. It may be advantageous to the school and to the life situation of a special group of students to start school an hour later than normal and finish in the afternoon an hour later than normal.

5. Another way to approach time-performance relationships is to adopt the *block* or *unit* system of delivering the timetable. This system has been known to improve attendance and virtually eliminate tardiness or latecomers.

Here is how it works:

In a semester, students work for unit packages of time averaging thirty-nine school days for each unit or block. In each block, students take only two courses or subjects. Each subject is taught for two and a half hours each day—one subject in the morning and the other in the afternoon. This allows school to start at 9:30 A.M. each day, giving students an extra half hour to arrive at school.

The thirty-nine-day span for the two subjects is easier for many students to relate to than a regular semester or year. They can see the completion of subjects in just about two calendar months. Students will come to school more often, and on time, if they can better see the results.

6. Many students are tardy because it is a hassle to get to their lockers for books each period. If the locker is at one end of the school and the classrooms scattered in every direction, it becomes difficult to reach the locker when books are needed. It is a good idea, therefore, if it is feasible in your situation, to encourage students to keep the morning or afternoon supply of books in book bags or briefcases they carry with them to class. Students normally place these book bags or other items underneath their desks when class is in session.

7. When students do come late to school, they should not be allowed an automatic entrance to class. Establish a formalized procedure whereby the late student must fill out an Admit to Class form (Figure 1-14). That form has a place for the student to write the reason for the tardiness.

70

Figure 1-14

ADMIT TO CLASS

ADMIT TO CLASS

Name _____ Date _____ Time _____

Reason for Lateness _____

_____

Consequences _____

_____

Student Signature _____ Teacher Signature _____

ADMIT TO CLASS

Name _____ Date _____ Time _____

Reason for Lateness _____

_____

Consequences _____

_____

Student Signature _____ Teacher Signature _____

AVOIDING PROBLEMS ON THE FIRST DAY OF SCHOOL

The first day back at school is often a traumatic event for students, as fears and anxieties, expectations, and rumors have developed concerning new teachers, new programs, and new students. It has been proven that this is one of the most stressful days for a student at school. This is especially true if that student has transferred from another school jurisdiction and all is new to him or her.

Those stressors may exist for students in the first day; however, stressors can be just as, or more, real for you, the teacher, on that day. Whether you are experienced in the school where you are now teaching or the assignment is new to you, there are strains and pressures to which you must adjust. The following basic rules have been carved out of the granite of experience for you to consider as you begin another—or your first—school year.

1. Greet the students at the door the first day, observe their deportment, and quickly separate any potential problem groups as they gravitate toward one another.

2. Before the first day, go through your class list and practice pronunciation of names, especially those foreign to you or ones that have a potential to be mispronounced. Know whether Ben prefers to be called Benny or Benjamin. If you do not have to ask which form he prefers, he will know you cared enough to find out.

3. Delve right into your subject first day, first thing. Establish your classroom procedures right away. This will keep the students alert. If you have an assignment associated with the presentation, it will give everyone something to work on while you collect fees and look after other logistics of the first day.

4. Watch your personal anger level. The stress of the first day back can occur because it is sometimes difficult to readjust to the classroom after a long stretch off; your frustration and tolerance levels may not be in a school mode. Do not burst out in anger at the first hint of a behavior problem.

    A little self-talk or mental preparation prior to the beginning of class is always a good idea. It will help you reestablish your mental set for working with students.

5. Many times on the first day, up to the grade 8 level, you may have a student who begins to cry. Be prepared; keep a box of tissues in your desk.

6. When you collect fees, make a point of not leaving the money in the classroom at any time. This money must go to the central office of the school immediately.

7. Watch for theft this first day. Many students have new materials in new bags and could become easy theft targets.

8. Use students who know the ins and outs of the school to show new students around.

9. Sincerely welcome any new staff member. Offer to be a help, not only with the procedures of the first day but with the rest of the year as well.

10. Review the code of ethics of your profession before you interact with the staff.

THE FIVE GREATEST FEARS OR CONCERNS OF PARENTS

Teachers and parents are partners in the education of children and they must work together for the maximum benefit of the child attending school. It therefore is of tremendous value to teachers at every grade level to understand what the major concerns of parents are when their children are in the school environment. Knowing the apprehensions of parents will give you an understanding base from which to view many parent actions. This is especially important as a child progresses through the school system and seeks out natural and normal ways of asserting independence.

The love and affection of the normal parent does not abate as the child searches for independence during the often turbulent days of adolescence. The mixed bag of caring, nurturing, and breaking away can serve to heighten the concerns or even fears of parents. Teachers must understand this if they are to be effective in communicating with students and parents.

The five fears or concerns of parents are:

1. Will their children be academically strong, with consistent good grades? As a child enters and works within the confines of a school, the average parent wants continuous success for that child.

   Parents can equate grades or marks with success in future life. Most parents feel that poor academic performance sometimes leads to other, more intense social and economic problems down the road.

2. Will their children fit in with the other students? Many parents understand that much of a child's happiness is a function of his or her peer relationships, and they may feel they have little or no control over those relationships.

   If a child becomes a "loner," that in itself is a problem. Positive peer relationships are seen by many to be a sign of normal social adjustment.

3. Will their children be abused by others at school? This fear or concern runs deep in all parents. The children they have protected and nurtured are now out of their physical protective care for five or more hours a day. We all hear on the news how violence is commonplace in our society. Parents wonder if some of that violence could affect their children while they are at school.

4. Will their children make friends with the wrong set of peers? Parents know how teenagers, especially, can be influenced by their friends. Many parents also feel that young people are often not mature enough to make logical, correct value judgments of others their age.

5. Will their children become involved with drugs or alcohol? Parents hear quite often of young people or of their dysfunctional rock star idols destroying themselves by overdosing on some chemical.

   Parents do not want to see a child they love, have worked for, taught, and planned for, throw his or her life away in a few hours because of poor decision making with regard to drugs.

When parents express these or any other concerns, lend a listening ear. Often, teachers can work together with parents to resolve some of the problems that give rise to these fears or concerns.

To alleviate many parent concerns, use a "Parent's Handbook," given at the beginning of the year to the parents of students new to your school. This book can address these and other problems. The handbook should show parents how school policies and procedures will resolve or handle the problems that exist. If parents understand that the school is an open partner with them in these areas, many fears will be lessened. Open communication is the key to understanding.

74

FIFTY SUICIDE INDICATORS—SYMPTOMS AND INSIGHTS

Much has been written about the suicide of young people. Because of the abhorrent nature of this phenomenon, the literature seeks to understand, to explain, and to prevent it from happening.

Unfortunately, no understanding or detail of explanation will do justice to the "why" question that is forever asked after a student takes his or her own life. That answer lies in the intricacy of the psychological makeup of the individual who commits it. When suicide occurs, the door to fully answering the "why" question is eternally shut.

Our purpose in this narrative is to prevent the "why" question from having to be asked in the first place. This can be accomplished only from knowledge of what to watch for. You'll find here as complete and comprehensive a list of suicide insights and indicators as possible.

Your position as a teacher is unique because you are working and interacting with the same people day in and day out. You can spot the changes in personality or see the indicators more clearly than any other member of society, other than a parent of the student.

Once you have identified a student at risk, notify the authorities at your school of your concerns. It then becomes their mandate to seek professional help for the student.

INDICATORS AND SYMPTOMS—THE WARNING SIGNS

1. Any mention of suicide or the mention of the thought of suicide.

2. A previous attempt at suicide.

3. A shutdown of interests—chronic disinterest in anything—a feeling of hopelessness.

4. The shunning of peers—wanting to be reclusive.

5. Depression from
   - a relationship breakup.
   - removal of peers.
   - family dysfunction.
   - abuse.

6. Increased interest in death and dying, expressed verbally or in written form.

7. Having had fundamental spiritual values usurped or discredited.

8. Sudden and abnormal deviations in behavior patterns.

9. Strong swings in mood—especially when there is no history of this in the child's life.

10. No motivation for physical activity—listless behavior.

11. Lack of concentration skills—inability to focus on one thing for any period of time.

75

12. Emotional outbursts with little, if any, provocation.

13. Alcohol or drug abuse.

14. Abnormal interest in suicide-victim rock star or teen idol.

15. The death of a close relative or friend.

16. Fear of the future of society.

17. Obsessive fear of failure.

18. Expression of being unloved.

19. Recognized mental illness—the student who seeks to escape from hallucinations or delusions.

20. Deep sense of personal isolation—the loner in a crowded school.

21. Periods of insomnia.

22. Periods of oversleeping.

23. Serious weight gain.

24. Loss of appetite.

25. Severe headaches.

26. Giving away prized possessions or making a last will.

27. Taking of unusual risks.

28. Dramatic changes in eating patterns.

29. Being HIV positive.

30. Trying to escape guilt—seen as an attempt to punish himself or herself.

31. Having had a close friend who committed suicide—copycat behavior.

INSIGHTS

32. More males commit suicide than females; however, more females attempt it.

33. Suicides tend to increase in springtime.

34. Many suicides are hidden in car accidents or are not reported as such by families.

35. Suicide occurs more often in urban areas than in rural areas.

36. Many people consume a substantial amount of drugs or alcohol in order to make it easier to perform the suicide act.

37. You do not need to have all the answers in order to talk the problem over with a potential suicide candidate.

38. The most common days for suicide are Monday and Tuesday.

39. Suicide is the second highest cause of death among adolescents.

40. The rate of suicide increases with age.

76

41. Suicide is less likely to occur if there are strong family and religious ties, as well as community involvement.

42. One of the worst periods for suicide is in the recovery stage from an illness.

43. Shooting or placing themselves in a situation where they are likely to be shot (robbing a bank) is the most common form of suicide among males.

44. The use of drugs is the most common form of suicide for females.

45. The most frequent time for suicide in depressed people is one hour before daybreak.

46. No social class is free from suicide. The taking of one's life is proportionally represented at all social levels.

47. Suicidal tendencies are not inherited. This should be stressed when counseling the child or sibling of a suicide victim.

48. The person who attempts suicide may see himself or herself as a burden to the family or society. This individual views himself or herself as not living up to expectations—and suicide pays the debt. The student who does not meet his or her parent's perceived academic expectations fits into this category.

49. The suicide attempt may be an attention-seeking mechanism or a cry for help. If someone is not satisfied with the attention or response to an attempt, he or she may try again and succeed.

50. The student may consider suicide as a form of revenge for some circumstance. He or she might say, "They'll be sorry when I'm gone."

➤ It is true that many of the suicide indicators or symptoms can occur quite apart from any desire to commit suicide. This will, of course, make it difficult for you to say that a particular student is or is not a potential candidate. It therefore is very important for you, the teacher in the classroom, to seek consultation with the school guidance counselor, psychologist, nurse, or other official if you observe any or several of the symptoms in a student.

GUIDELINES FOR DEALING WITH STUDENTS WHO SKIP SCHOOL (AN ATTENDANCE POLICY)

One of the major problems teachers and administrators have is maintaining regular attendance at school and school-related activities. In our society, the majority of students do not skip but some students—for one reason or another—do not have the maturity to predict the very real consequences of an incomplete education.

Each individual student is different, and so are the circumstances. Some students are victims of social and economic situations (abuse, etc.) that cause them to see attendance at school as secondary to their attempts to cope with the environment they live in. Whatever the cause of poor school attendance, that skipping, in turn, creates three basic problems for teachers.

1. When a student is absent, he or she is missing a certain amount of work that may have to be retaught.

2. If you let a student get away with little or no consequence for being absent, other students will soon imitate the behavior.

3. When a student skips school, he or she is certain to be tardy in terms of handing in assignments. You therefore may find yourself in a position of playing "catch-up" when it comes to having all the necessary term marks for this student.

The school itself, aside from all other considerations, must function to fulfill the rights to an education of the majority who are not skipping and sincerely want to better themselves through your institution. To clearly define the parameters of attendance expectations for these and others, a practical attendance policy is needed in every school. The following is a model of such a policy as it relates to the middle, junior high, or high school levels.

1. Regular attendance is the personal responsibility of every student. It is the student's responsibility to match or conform his or her behavior to the attendance expectations of the school in order to meet the student's personal and societal (administration) goals of education.

2. The school is responsible to encourage regular attendance and to monitor the attendance patterns, to inform parents and students of attendance problems, and to provide a process to improve attendance if this becomes necessary.

3. The student's role is to make a commitment to attend school and classes on time, on a regular basis.

4. In the event a student is to be absent from school, the parent, guardian, or student living on his or her own is required to contact the school in reasonable time (usually the morning before school) and provide an explanation as to why the student will be absent.

5. When a student absence is not explained by the parent or guardian, the absence is to be recorded as unexcused (a skip).

6. The school will tolerate three unexcused absences (skips) in individual classes the student is registered in before a consultation meeting with the student, the parent or guardian, and a member of the school administration is convened. Two unexcused absences after that meeting may result in the student's being removed from the individual class.

   If, however, a student has reached a total of nine unexcused absences in a term or designated time period, even without three in one particular class, the student, parent or guardian, and a member of the school administration shall have a consultation meeting. If there are three skips after this meeting, it becomes the prerogative of the school administration and the school board whether the student shall be removed from the school for a period of time.

7. It is the responsibility of the student to catch up with any classroom work missed during any student absence. Teachers may refuse to accept late assignments or to provide makeup exams for students with unexcused absences.

The attendance policy at any school must be workable and fair. This means that there should be a certain amount of room for teacher or administration discretion built into the system to allow for those variables in student's lives that can have a devastating effect on their attendance. The breakup of a family is a good example of this. Compassion, tempered with fair firmness, should be the guiding principle.

HOW TO HAVE A PRODUCTIVE MEETING WITH THE PARENTS OF A BEHAVIOR-PROBLEM CHILD

Some students are behavior problems, and it is often necessary to bring in the parents of that child to discuss behavior and future plans for student success.

Most parents welcome the opportunity to have direct contact with teachers who are working with their children. Parents want things to go smoothly for their children and recognize, as you do, that parent-teacher relationships should be as positive and highly communicative as possible.

GUIDELINES FOR A PRODUCTIVE MEETING

1. The main objective of a meeting with the parent of any student should be to maximize educational benefits for that child.

2. It is also important that you and the parents carry away no emotional baggage after the meeting. Confrontations, strong disagreements, and hot tempers have no place at this type of gathering.

3. Be prepared. Gather as much written evidence about the behavior of the child as possible.

4. Discuss details ahead of time with other teachers. Have other teachers present if you feel it is necessary.

5. You may find it necessary to suspend the student in order to bring the parent in.

6. Start the meeting with a positive comment after the initial greetings.

7. List the evidence gathered from other teachers:
   ➠ Stress evidence that is nonrefutable.
   ➠ Stress repeated offenses.
   ➠ State number, not names, of witnesses until necessary to do so.

8. Ask the student to speak to the wrongs.

9. Refuse to accept statements in which the child blames others for obvious wrongs.

10. Ask the parents to speak to the wrongs.

11. Suggest an effective plan of action with options, for example:
    ➠ Suspension for a day
    ➠ Work in isolation, if permitted by school board
    ➠ Contracts (stress the need for commitment here)
    ➠ Retribution—payback for damages, apologies, and so forth

12. Ask the student to agree to the action plan. It is important that the student have ownership of the problem and the solution to the problem.

13. Find something positive to say about the student as he or she leaves the meeting.

14. Support the development of an alternate school program if there are several chronic-behavior-problem students in your school or school jurisdiction. This program will act as a pressure release valve for the average classroom teacher who must work with up to forty students in today's classrooms.

80

GUIDELINES FOR DEALING WITH BOMB THREATS

The possibility of a bomb threat at your school is a genuine reality these days. The reasons a person phones in a bomb threat are many and varied. Some dysfunctional person may be getting a distorted thrill from seeing a school evacuated, or a student or two may just want to get an instant holiday or miss a test or quiz.

Each school must have a bomb threat policy to protect the students, deter any recurrences of this problem, and minimize disruption of classroom routines.

The following guidelines should be part of any policy in this area:

1. The bomb threat may arrive by any means including letters or anonymous notes. Most threats are made to the school, of course, by telephone. It therefore is important that the school subscribe to a caller ID system from the telephone company. It is also a good idea to have access to a recording system, activated by the push of a button, for the telephone.

2. If the threat arrives by mail or note, every effort should be made by the person reading the statement not to touch or handle the correspondence once the threat is realized.

3. Bomb-making instructions have been available through the Internet for some time. This increases the likelihood of your having one in the school building. In the event a suspicious-looking package is found in the school building, evacuation procedures must be started immediately. There is no room for hesitation in decision making.

4. Evacuation should be rehearsed and must proceed with the same efficiency as for a fire drill.

5. A central location or communications center, such as the principal's office, should be the hub of incoming and outgoing information on the threat once it has occurred.

6. When a bomb threat is initially received, a code should be given over the intercom. This gives teachers and support persons the opportunity to immediately search their own area for packages or unusual objects while not alarming the student population. This must be done because, in a worst—case scenario, a bomb would be in the evacuation path of your students. Teachers should also have an "all clear" or "package located" signal that is sent to the office by way of the intercom.

7. When the bomb threat code is sent to the classrooms, those teachers or support staff who are available to help with a search should report to the central office or information center immediately.

8. Teachers and support staff should be instructed on how to handle an incoming bomb threat phone call. This is especially important if there is no recording device in the school's telephone system. Include the following in those instructions:

 Try to remember the exact wording of the threat. Note accents, speech problems, and background noise. Write it down if you can.

➧ Identify the sex of the caller.

➧ Judge the maturity level of the person.

➧ Do not interfere with what the person is saying. Decide if he or she is loud or soft, fast or slow, and what the emotional state of the person is.

➧ Get as many details as possible:
   – When is it set to explode?
   – Where is it in the school?
   – What type of bomb is it (pipe, bag, etc.)?

➧ Jot down the date and time of the call.

➧ Ask the person his or her name and where he or she is. Believe it or not, the person will sometimes blurt this out.

9. The principal or designate, of course, should immediately call the police.

10. The entire building should be searched with the aid of the police.

11. In most cases, it is necessary to evacuate the students as the call comes in. This may be playing into the power-seeking thrill of the perpetrator, however, as that person quite often is watching the school from a distance for this very reaction. In some situations, a bomb threat routine involving the school gym can be used; all students are evacuated to the school gymnasium after the gym itself has been thoroughly searched. Once the rest of the school has been completely examined and cleared by the police, students can then return to classes. Whatever the case, the safety of the students and staff is the top priority. Consultation and instruction should be part of an in-service for the staff from the local police or other government agency. This should all dovetail with board policies to minimize the problem.

82

39

THE JUNIOR JANITOR PROGRAM

Many times, when teachers are on supervision, at recess or noon hour, they run into serious and not-so-serious breaches of school rules and proper conduct procedures. There is often little a teacher can do but verbally reprimand the individuals involved or send them to some higher authority. What teachers need is an effective deterrent for improper or hurtful behavior that occurs on almost every schoolyard.

The deterrent must, of course, fit the offense, and therefore some choice should be involved. The Junior Janitor idea allows for just that. Using this plan, a student's errant behavior on the schoolyard is seen as "volunteering" to do community service around the school by becoming a junior janitor. For example, if Betty is seen to cause trouble, she is sent to the "Junior Janitor Board." She then has to choose the task she has "volunteered" for. On the board is a list of tasks that always need to be completed around any school. Jobs such as sweeping the gym floor, picking up papers, and putting away library books are good examples. The Junior Janitor Board works well because the student chooses the janitor job. Complaints are fewer and work gets done.

The Junior Janitor Board itself should be in a high-profile location in the school where students can see new items that are placed on the board each week. This keeps the consequences for poor behavior in a student's mind at all times.

Like many sanctions in the real world, it is a more socially accepted thing to do community service, which benefits all, than to have a personal punishment that only negatively affects the student, and from which nobody really benefits.

THE STUDENT CONNECTION PROCESS—
A TEACHER-TO-OFFICE COMMUNICATION,
SUPPORT, AND DISCIPLINE SYSTEM

Some students will be serious behavior problems in the classroom. This situation, combined with the consciousness of human rights and the fear of abuse that is uppermost in the minds of the public, makes it necessary for teachers at the classroom level to have access to an effective discipline policy. That policy must not be coercive or demeaning in any way; it must lead to a positive, well-run learning environment. That learning environment is indeed possible to attain and maintain through strong teacher-to-school office communications and interaction, combined with a policy of mutual support and respect.

A fundamental series of problems occurs when a student chooses to become a behavior problem at the classroom level.

These include:

1. In many jurisdictions, the teacher cannot leave the classroom filled with students in order to escort the child to the office, nor can the student be sent unsupervised to the office.

2. The office staff in many cases will not know the nature of the problem when that student arrives at the office.

3. Frequently there is no "cooling down" process through which the student can describe his or her point of view.

4. There is often no formal process where information about the student and the problem can be expanded to reveal underlying causative factors.

5. Teacher-to-office communication is restricted by virtue of distance and the fact that the teacher is presenting a lesson at the time.

With the Student Connection Process, the serious-behavior-problem student must be sent to the office. If your school does not allow a student to go alone to the office, then a teacher aide or other designated person should be made available to be summoned by the teacher to escort the student to the office.

It is imperative that the student be removed from his or her peer audience at the classroom level. Once the student has gone to the office, the teacher must fill in the Quick Details Form (Figure 1-15). This easily completed teacher-friendly form lists thirty-one behavior problems that could occur in the average classroom. As the teacher, you simply check off the appropriate listed behaviors that apply to the student in question. Included at the bottom of the form is a space called "More Quick Details" where you can expand on the problem.

The Quick Details Form is then sent in a sealed envelope with the escort (or by runner) to the office. This will instantly inform the powers that be of the nature of the problem that is causing at the class level.

Once the student is in the office, she or he is given the Student Connection Form (Figure 1-16). This two-page form connects the student to the problem by asking the basic questions of what, why, who, and how.

84

© 1998 by The Center for Applied Research in Education

The first question on the first page asks the student what the problem is from his or her point of view. The second question asks the student what events led up to the problem, and the third question seeks out the involvement of others.

Questions 4, 5, and 6, while they also seek facts from the student, cause the student to connect with ownership of the problem. Question 4 asks why the student chose to act the way he or she did.

Question 5 asks the student to find some method to resolve or fix the problem so he or she can return to class.

Question 6 is the "game plan" question. In this question, the student must set forth a plan on how to behave, so there will not be a recurrence of the problem.

After the office staff have reviewed the paperwork the student has completed, they will then interview the child to build up a further data base.

The teacher in the classroom is then communicated with and allowed to review all the information collected, and a mutual decision on the consequences for the behavior is developed between the teacher and the office administrative staff. A decision on whether to consult the parents of the behavior-problem student is also made at this time. The consequences the child must face are to be a function of the local school board policies as they relate to the nature of the problem the child created in the classroom. It may be mandatory in some jurisdictions to return the student to the classroom immediately, no matter what the errant behavior was. If this is the case, that policy must be taken into consideration when decisions about the consequences are made.

The overall advantages of the Student Connection Process go beyond the actual resolution of the problem. These advantages include:

1. A paper trail is set up with which the student and the teacher describe the situation. This creates a valuable written record of the problem.

2. Not only is the student caused to have ownership of the problem he or she has created, but that student has input into the solution to that problem.

3. The student is removed from his or her peer audience, thereby maintaining order in the classroom.

4. The student is dealt with in a noncoercive manner that works for her or his ultimate benefit.

5. Interactive communication takes place between the teacher and the office staff. This is a regular system of consistent support.

6. Students will know there is a support mechanism in place to back up teachers. This, in itself, will deter many poor behaviors.

7. A "cooling down" of the student's emotional state occurs when he or she is required to focus on and fill in the Student Connection Form.

The Student Connection Process is a way for teachers and school administration officials to work together to solve discipline problems. It relies heavily on interactive communication, mutual decision making, respect, and support. This combination of factors must be in place and functioning if the teacher is to effectively perform in today's classroom environment.

Figure 1-15

QUICK DETAILS FORM

Date: _____   Time of Incident _____

Student's Name: _____

Check off the behaviors you have observed:

_____ stealing	_____ shooting objects
_____ swearing	_____ spit balls
_____ lying	_____ throwing objects
_____ fighting	_____ smoking
_____ direct abuse of others	_____ lighting matches
_____ spitting	_____ using obscene gestures
_____ cheating	_____ excessive disruptions
_____ odor of alcohol	_____ refusal to be on task
_____ excessive talking	_____ refusal to be cooperative
_____ talking back to teacher	_____ pushing/shoving
_____ intimidation (bullying)	_____ use of objects as weapons
_____ sexual harassment	_____ possession of a knife
_____ use of threats	_____ sleeping
_____ vandalism (willful destruction of property)	_____ leaving classroom without permission
_____ racist remarks	_____ making excessive noise
_____ racist notes	_____ others

More Quick Details:

_____

_____

_____

_____

_____

Teacher Signature

Figure 1-16

STUDENT CONNECTION FORM

Name: _____   Date: _____   Time: _____

1) Please describe what the situation or problem is as you see it.

_____

_____

_____

2) What events led up to the problem? What happened before the problem to make the problem occur?

_____

_____

_____

3) Who else was involved? Were there any witnesses? Please name these people and describe what they did.

_____

_____

_____

Figure 1-16 *(continued)*
STUDENT CONNECTION FORM

4) Why did you choose to act the way you did?

_____

_____

_____

5) How can you resolve or fix this problem so you can return to class?

_____

_____

_____

6) The Game Plan Question ⟹ Please describe how you plan to behave so you do not cause this problem to happen again.

_____

_____

_____

41 **WHAT TO DO AND WHAT NOT TO DO WHEN YOU SEE A PERSON WITH A GUN IN SCHOOL**

In this society, the number of socially or emotionally dysfunctional people entering schools or other public service establishments with a gun is on the increase. Unfortunately, there have been deadly examples of unprovoked shootings of innocent children and teachers in many places. No school or neighborhood is completely free of deranged individuals.

There is no set pattern of behaviors or psychological profiles that will allow you to quickly identify this type of deviant. The rules of normal logic do not apply. The assailant could be suffering from one of many psychological disorders or be driven by a drug-induced psychosis. Indeed, it is not uncommon for an attacker to have no relationship with the school or its staff and students. Rational thought is not taking place.

It has been recognized that persons carrying weapons into the school will fall into one of five categories. These are:

1. The person who is serious and has decided beforehand to kill someone. This quite often ends in murder, and—in many cases—suicide.

2. The person who is seeking an excuse to use the weapon. He or she is looking for even the slightest provocation to start shooting.

3. The showoff.

4. Gang-related power or vendetta.

5. Self-defense.

The following guidelines help you know what to do and what not to do if this problem occurs at your school.

1. If a person (student or otherwise) threatens to get a gun or to shoot one of the staff or students, take this threat seriously and send the police to stop the person and to provide the school with security until the person is located and dealt with.

2. If you encounter a person with an offensive weapon in the school, assume that he or she is serious and is determined to do harm. Do not minimize the problem, even if you know the person very well.

3. Panicking is a luxury you cannot afford. If you panic, you will be a detriment to yourself and the students. In fact, your calmness may be your best defense. You may feel anger or fear on the inside, but you must not show this.

4. Try to reduce the number of people at risk to a minimum. If it is at all possible to remove the children and yourself from the path of the person with the weapon, do so. This is best done by telling the children to follow the fire escape plan and to meet at some neutral spot that is safe.

5. If confronted, speak in a low, steady, calm, nonthreatening voice. Plant ideas in the assailant's mind. Statements like "You don't want to hurt the innocent children," "We can help you out of this," or "You are not a bad person" will help calm down the aggressor. Encourage verbalization from the person. He or she is less likely to shoot when talking, and it will give you more information to work with.

6. Develop a code system for the school intercom. The logic here is to use "Code 7" because the letter G of Gun is the seventh letter of the alphabet. The codes can, of course, go both ways. If a teacher sees a person in the school with a weapon, this information can be transmitted to the office by the code and, as the office finds out, it can inform the rest of the school.

7. The staff should have an in-service on this topic presented by local law enforcement officials.

8. If shots have been fired in the hall or in another room, and you cannot get out of your classroom, have the students kneel down and face the inside wall that is on the same side as the door. Tell the students to put their heads between their knees. This will limit the assailant's view and recognition of the children in case he or she has come to single out a particular student. This position against the wall will help keep students out of the line of fire if the attacker decides to shoot.

9. If you know the person, use the personal history that you are aware of to your advantage.

10. Do not ask the person to give it (the gun) to you.

11. Do not run after the person with a gun.

12. Do not yell, scream, or otherwise try to intimidate the assailant, who will see this as a verbal threat or the needed provocation.

13. If you overpower the person with a gun, you must completely immobilize him or her, because you do not know what other weaponry he or she may have.

90

THE THIRTY-FIVE MINUTE SOLUTION

Behavior control can take many forms. The school administration must find the best policies or methods of managing schools in order to create efficient and safe learning environments. One area often overlooked, in terms of discipline, is the amount of time spent at the noon-hour break. To minimize fights, squabbles, and other associated problems, shorten the noon hour to a maximum of thirty-five minutes. This thirty-five-minute time frame is sufficient for students and staff to eat lunch and blow off a little steam.

You will find that this shortened noon hour works best when the majority of your students do not go home for lunch. If this is the case in your school, and your school jurisdiction and staff will allow the change, you will benefit from the following four distinct advantages of the shortened noon hour.

1. Many students tend to get bored after about twenty minutes to half an hour with whatever activity or game they are playing in the schoolyard. This is when pushing, shoving, and name calling cause tempers to rise. The thirty-five-minute noon hour nips these problems in the bud.

2. You offer less opportunity to outside influences (drug dealers, etc.) to contact or have an effect on the students.

3. The students can be released from school approximately one-half hour earlier.

4. There is less downtime between being released at noon and returning to classes after lunch. It becomes less difficult to reestablish a "motivational set" with students on projects or assignments that were started before noon. This gives greater continuity to the school day.

THE PROJECT SHOP
(A UNIQUE, YET EFFECTIVE, BEHAVIOR-CONTROL IDEA)

Some students in your school have a high potential to become behavior problems. These students are usually, but not always, from problem families—perhaps where parents are not in place—or they may be from families that are overly permissive.

Many of these students need ways to channel their energies in order to control their behavior. These students can often be seen shoving and jostling others in the hall and challenging your authority in the classroom.

A unique way to direct the aggression or energy of this type of student is to start a "Project Shop" for him or her. You will need a classroom or some other small space, if there is one. In this area, you set up a number of tables that can take a scratch or two. On each table, place a small mechanical device, such as an old clock, radio, television set (remove the picture tube), or lawn mower motor (no gasoline).

These projects can be easily obtained with a small ad in the newspaper, or they may be donated by people you know; everyone seems to have an old clock or radio lying around. You want a number of projects that students can work on or, more likely, just take apart to see what makes them tick. Many behavior-problem students are not strong in the academic areas but are good with tactile skills, so it follows that these students will be strongly drawn to the "Project Shop." In the event that students do actually repair some of the items, this is a bonus, as the items can then be sold to buy more items to work on.

The tools you require can be obtained with a phone call to a service club, or again from donations through a simple ad in the newspaper. Garage sales and pawn shops will often have a large selection of screwdrivers, pliers, and wrenches of every size at very low prices.

The only problem with this idea will be how to keep the students out of the project room. This is best accomplished with tickets. Students can be allowed to work on the projects only if they have a project or shop ticket; you decide who gets to work on the motors and other projects. The right to work on the projects can be used as a reward for positive behavior in the classroom—creating a beneficial impact in the classroom.

One school that has the project shop in full operation does not have a spare room for the students to work in. They simply placed five 4-foot by 8-foot tables in a low-traffic area of the hall and had students work there. When students had to return to classes, their projects and tools were placed in boxes underneath the tables, out of harm's way. In that particular school, behavior problems were significantly reduced.

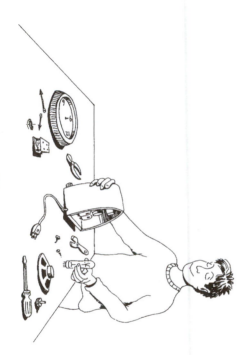

92

44

GUIDELINES FOR DEALING WITH FIGHTS AT SCHOOL

Often, teachers and administrators are working with young people who are immature and therefore lacking in developed social skills. Because of that immaturity, their behavior patterns do not fit neatly into theories or philosophical stances.

Many of these students' behaviors are unpredictable. At one minute, a student will exhibit perfectly rational, mature behavior when working in class, then go out into the schoolyard at recess shortly thereafter and immediately get into a fist-fight. A large number of students have not yet learned to maintain a consistent level of normal actions and reactions. This situation is complicated by the fact that some students have difficulties with social environments or peer relations.

A few of these students will get into fights or acts of violence for sheer excitement; for other students, aggression is almost a lifestyle. They have learned that the negative attention they draw is better than no attention at all. When the fight-oriented student attends school, the school or school system must curtail or restrain that aggressive behavior within its legal jurisdiction.

The following guidelines will help you discourage and prevent fighting. The basic approaches—like providing adequate supervision, verbal reprimands, suspensions, and detention programs—are understood. These guidelines go beyond the basics to provide you with some unique insights and novel ways of dealing with fights.

1. If you catch students misbehaving and perceive that this could lead to a fight, have two quarantine areas of the school or school yard where they are to go for time out. With each participant in a different area, tempers will cool.

2. Watch for abnormal congregations of students; break them up. Students will not usually come and tell a supervisor of an impending fight. They become excited at the prospect of a fight and promote it through a kind of mob mentality.

3. Identify potential fighters before there is a problem. Seek counseling or anger management instruction for these students. This is where a good anecdotal record of the child's behavior patterns will be of great benefit to you.

4. Watch for students with odd names. Some parents think it is cute to give their children unusual names at birth (e.g., Candy Barr). Studies have shown that a child is continually embarrassed by the odd name and builds up a sense of resentment about it because a name is an easy target for mocking or teasing. This is reflected in behavior, as the child with the strange name is up to 40 percent more likely to cause problems in school and later commit a crime.

5. Have your local police speak to each class on the topic of violence in the school. Many people think it is ineffective at the high school level, but that is not so. The real-world consequences of assault and violence are of concern to the upper-grade-level student.

6. In health class, impress upon the students the newest threat involved in fighting. If students hit or scratch another and draw blood, they are possibly exposing themselves to AIDS or hepatitis.

93

7. Fights anywhere in the school should be reported immediately to the school office. It does not pay to delay action, as the situation surrounding a problem tends to become blurred in people's memories even after an hour or two.

8. Do not break up a fight when you are alone unless there is no other person available to help you. There should normally be a minimum of two staff members to break up a fight.

9. When breaking up the fight, dominate the fight situation with your voice. Do not touch the participants with your bare hands, and watch out for body fluids. If any body fluids do get on you, wash them off immediately.

10. It may be advantageous to make watching a fight a breach of school rules, with resultant consequences.

11. Produce a no-fight-zone school policy, with effective consequences that all will know of and that will be consistently enforced. If the students know there is strength behind the policy, it will be easier to enforce.

12. Have a mediation meeting between the two fighting individuals. It teaches students other methods of conflict resolution.

94

45 WHAT TO DO WHEN YOU ARE PHYSICALLY ATTACKED BY A STUDENT

Increasingly, teachers, principals, and support staff are being physically attacked by students or students' family members. The reasons for these attacks are as varied as are the people who perpetrate them.

Some generalizations have been cited as root causes of this behavior. These include the increase in violence on television and the general decay of the moral structures of society. These reasons are indeed operational, but knowing them does little to help you in the case of attack, other than to make you aware that you should be prepared for it.

The following list of ideas will help. These ideas go beyond the obvious, like calling the police, running away from the attacker, or simply shouting for help.

1. Maintain presence of mind; do not go limp. Some people, when they are attacked, faint or fall into a state of shock, but you must avoid this if at all possible.

2. If the problem is chronic in your area, wear a personal alarm device.

3. Many attacks on teachers occur in the parking lot. If you suspect a problem, leave the school with other teachers. It may be to your advantage to have a remote starting system installed in your vehicle to speed up departure from the parking lot.

4. Call for your staff to be given an in-service on one of the many attack defense programs now available.

5. After the attack, talk it over with a colleague and tape-record this conversation.

6. If you are not too upset by the attack, write down the totality of the event immediately; use the tape-recorded conversation to help you. You should include the events leading up to the problem, what was said, positions of people at the time, witnesses, time of day, facial expressions of the people, and what actually transpired during the process of the attack.

7. Tap into the resources of your professional association or employer, or search out a community crisis center for help.

8. Get medical attention immediately, even if the attack was slight. Symptoms may not show up for some time. Make sure the school office has a record of the event and any injuries to you. This is especially important in terms of litigation and compensation.

9. Remember that the psychological damage from an attack can often be as traumatic as physical abuse—or even more so. Do not minimize this damage to you or to a colleague.

10. Carry through with any criminal charges to be laid. If the aggressor is allowed to get away without paying the correct legal consequences, then you and your colleagues will be more at risk.

11. If you see the physical abuse coming, put your arms (not your hands) directly up in front of your face, in much the same way as a boxer does to avoid blows to the front of his body. Your head should be slightly tucked into your arms. You will notice that as you do this, your elbows protect your chest area as well.

12. If someone grabs your arm, the automatic tendency is to push against that person. This is the wrong thing to do. You will not break away from the grasp of a person by pushing. Look at the position of the attacker's hand and pull your arm away from where the thumb meets the index finger; this is the weakest point in the grip. The other way to break a grip is to pull up with your other hand on the ring finger of the aggressor. Practice these two simple maneuvers so you will immediately know what to do if the time comes.

13. Scream as loudly as possible.

96

46

SEVEN WAYS TO MAKE SURE HOMEWORK GETS COMPLETED

Homework can be a critical part of school life. It is an extension of the work performed in the classroom—a necessary reality. Students may not see it this way, and some may try to avoid the extra work. Parents, for the most part, are supportive of their children having homework, and are pleased to see a child complete an assignment and do well.

The following guidelines will help you make sure that homework gets finished and returned to you.

1. Create a "homework policy" for your classroom (if your school does not already have one). This policy should be sent home to the parents of every student. In this policy letter, set out clear-cut guidelines about what you expect in terms of:

   ➥ Amount of time normally to be spent on homework assignments for your grade level.

   ➥ Technical details you require (e.g., page numbers at the start of each math assignment, or bibliographies for all essays or reports).

   ➥ What to do if homework cannot be completed due to circumstances (e.g., send a note, phone secretary at school).

2. Have students sign for homework pages that you have numbered. This way no student can say, "I never received the material or the homework to do."

3. Make the completion of homework worth a percentage of the term mark.

4. When you give out homework sheets, have a space at the bottom for a parent to sign. Then, a parent can't complain, "My Judy never gets any homework! Why is this?"

5. Some parents have their children involved in community activities of every sort, and those activities frequently interfere with homework. To help overcome this problem, give out homework assignments that are due, not the next day, but in two or three days' time. Make sure you write on the assignment the date assigned and the date due. Have the student sign his or her name beside this information.

6. Be sensitive to what other teachers are doing or have assigned. If Mrs. Smith down the hall is giving your home class a major science test tomorrow, it may not be judicious for you to give a large homework assignment to those same students tonight. A little cooperation and communication with that other teacher will go a long way toward making things easier for everyone.

DEALING WITH THE BACK-TALKING STUDENT

The student who talks back to you in a belligerent or challenging way can be a problem at any level of teaching. This impudent child is not created in a vacuum; usually he or she is a victim of verbal abuse, has missed some areas of developmental reasoning, or is from a problematic family situation. While teaching thirty-plus students, you are not going to be able to instantly solve the psychological problems of the back-talking student. You need resolution now, as this student is defying—or even mocking—you in the classroom.

Included here are two lists to help you deal with this problem. The first list contains some further insights, and the second list offers helpful techniques.

INSIGHTS

1. The worst kind of back-talking occurs when you are challenged in the process of making a presentation. Typically, the student will say something like "Who cares about this junk," "What's the point of this?" or "This stuff sucks." The student is clearly trying to intimidate you. This type of defiance in itself is gratifying for the student, as he or she thinks about getting some admiration from peers for having the bravado to take you on. This is one reason why your threatening consequences is of little value at this point.

2. When a student talks back to you, you actually have three problems:

   ➤ The student is refusing to do the work.

   ➤ He or she is distracting you and probably the entire class from the lesson.

   ➤ The student is trying to usurp your authority.

3. If you shout at the student, you have just entered into a power struggle you may well lose. Some students will just shout back at you.

4. The back-talk response will come when you least want it, but it will come from the student from whom you most expect it.

5. Most back-talk behavior is for attention-seeking purposes.

TECHNIQUES THAT HELP

1. Spot the problem before class begins. Isolate the potential back-talkers and instruct them on what you will tolerate and what you will not.

2. Have zero tolerance for back-talking. Send the student to the office immediately or signal for office personnel to come and escort the student away from your classroom.

3. The school office should have a good working policy to handle student defiance of teachers, such as the student connection process that places ownership of the problem where it belongs—with the student.

98

4. Voice control is important. Speak in a calm but firm manner. This will minimize your risk of getting into a power struggle. By not reacting aggressively or showing signs of hurt or lack of composure, you will not give power to the student; the student will see that he or she never "got to you."

5. In the younger grades, if the situation as you perceive it is not extremely serious and you can see that this student simply needs a little "direction," use the volleyball card system. The first time the student talks back to you, give him or her a yellow card; the second time it happens, give a second yellow card. The third time it happens, give the student a red card that has a reasonably serious consequence written on it for the student to perform. This method of control is usually quite effective. You do not even need to stop your lesson presentation. Simply give the student the card and continue your work. Students will know that you mean business as you carry out the consequence.

6. If the problem seems to be chronic in a particular class, separate the students into circular groups of three to five students. Place the potential back-talkers or behavior problems with a group that will not feed their egos. Make sure the problem student is situated so that he or she cannot have easy contact with peers.

While it is true that dealing with the back-talking student is one of the most difficult areas of teaching to "get a handle on," it can be accomplished quite successfully. You do not have to be a 300-pound fire breather to control students in the modern classroom. You do have to have strength of character and personally strong emotional resources to be able to set the proper quality behavior standards for your class.

A personal note here: The best behavior control and classroom manager I have ever come across was Mother Edith. She was a top-notch high school English teacher in a rough-and-tumble boys' school. She always received assignments from her boys on time, student behavior was 100 percent under control, and you could hear a butterfly flying by outside her classroom when she wanted quiet. I knew her when she was nearing sixty years of age. You see, what made Mother Edith unique was that she was only about three feet, five inches tall. She was short of stature, but there was ten feet of power in that woman!

GUIDELINES FOR DEALING WITH A CHALLENGING PARENT

Some parents will challenge you on a particular issue—a point of discipline, grades, or your teaching style. In addition, some parents think their children are perfect in every way—can do no wrong—and anything negative associated with their children is someone else's fault. A parent may also challenge you rather than face his or her own child, who is the cause of the problem.

When you recognize that you have a challenging parent—one who fits the above criteria, or worse—refer to the following set of guidelines:

1. Don't make light of or trivialize a parent's concern. To him or her, this is a major, real problem.

2. If an angry parent comes to you, try not to buy into that anger. If you return anger for anger, in addition to accomplishing nothing for the child, you will give more credence to the parent's challenging point of view.

3. Let the parent vent his or her whole concern before you speak; do not interrupt.

4. If you feel the situation is serious enough, have another teacher or school official present as a witness.

5. When it is your turn to talk, speak in a low monotone to help calm down everyone, including yourself.

6. Ask the parent and the student (if present) questions to clarify the situation. Many times, contradictions will show up at this point.

7. Avoid making the situation or problem into a "power" issue. You are concerned only about the child's education and success.

8. Be prepared. Your best defense is to have complete documentation on the child and the situation. Keep a file on this student as soon as you recognize the potential for trouble. Have all students sign for assignments and keep accurate, up-to-date records.

9. Make notes while the parent and others are speaking. This gives you time to think, and it will relax you, as well as give you data to refer back to in the meeting.

10. If you are in error, admit it. This will often resolve the situation immediately.

11. If you are not wrong and the child is at fault, do not be self-sacrificing and accept blame in order to resolve the situation quickly.

12. Work through a solution while the child is there or when the parent is ready to accept a solution.

13. Watch out for the intimidation factor. Some parents will try to bully you physically by entering your personal space or by making physical contact. If this happens, shut the meeting down immediately. Leave the room. Do whatever you must do to avoid physical intimidation. This situation can obviously lead to larger problems, and is another reason to have a colleague or school official as a witness. Report these circumstances to your supervisor at once.

14. Once you have completed the meeting with the challenging parent, write everything down, including the behavior of the child and parent. Write down any plans for the resolution of problems. Sign and date the document and give a copy to your supervisor.

49 ## SELF-DISCIPLINE GUIDELINES FOR TEACHERS

In every profession, there are circumstances, people, and things that may cause stress, anxiety of all sorts, and downright grief. Teaching is no different from other professions. Many of these situations are self-induced—or at least subject to your personal control in some way or another. Listed here are twelve rules that you must adhere to if you are to handle the rigors of the modern classroom. Follow these stress-reducing precepts that have been hammered out on the anvil of experience.

1. Quit smoking. All the evidence is in.

2. Get enough exercise. Walk at least forty minutes five times a week. Also, when everyone tries to get the classroom on the ground floor (usually at the start or end of a school year)—*don't*. If you can, have your classroom on the top floor of the school. This has two distinct advantages:

   a. Cardiologists have proven that if you walk up six flights of stairs a day, you will have an improved cardiovascular system.

   b. Fewer people will come up to you with nonessential requests, obligations, and hassles, because they have to walk up the stairs.

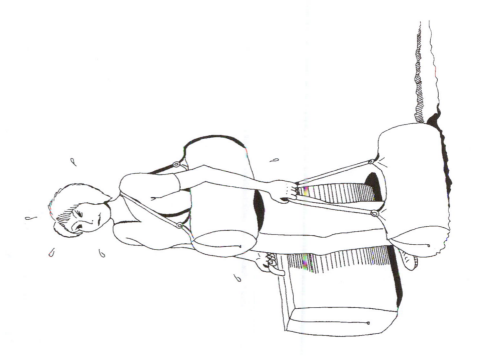

3. Get enough sleep. Avoid stress-producing television shows or movies before sleeping.

4. Do not let the sun set while you have unresolved anger as a result of interaction with a colleague or student. Try your best to resolve the problem as early in the day as possible.

5. Avoid talking negatively about a student while you are in the staff room or elsewhere. Some of those negative comments can become self-fulfilling prophecies.

6. Shut your school day down at a decent time of day. Leave the school. Go home.

7. Find some kind of frustration pressure valve for yourself when you are in the heat of a disagreement with a behavior-problem student. Discipline yourself to count to ten . . . as many times as it takes to do the job.

8. Do not take on extra baggage. If a family comes to you needing resolution of a social problem that affects their child but does not really fall within your mandate as a teacher, DO NOT TAKE IT ON. Direct the family to qualified social workers or social service agencies.

9. Be sure you do not buy into another person's anger over a student or situation.

10. Try not to compare your teaching style with that of Mrs. Jones down the hall. Maybe she's God's gift to teaching and "the kids just love her," but what works for someone else may not work for you. You must develop your own workable style; make your classroom your own, not a copy of someone else's.

102

50

FIFTY WAYS TO DISCOURAGE AND PREVENT CHEATING IN THE CLASSROOM

Some students cheat. This has been a fact of school life from the start. It is in the nature of some students to try to beat the system, and they can be very creative in the process. Cheating is a difficult habit for a student to break because of the sporadic reinforcement associated with it. Students, on occasion, will even work harder at cheating than would be necessary for them to study for the test or do the work in the first place.

The following guidelines will help you become aware of areas where cheating can occur before, during, and after a test:

1. Do not allow the test to be written with erasable pens or pencils.

2. Before giving a test, turn the desks to face the wall and push them up to the chalkboard as much as possible.

3. Have students switch desks, not just move desks away from each other. This avoids notes being taped to the bottom of desks.

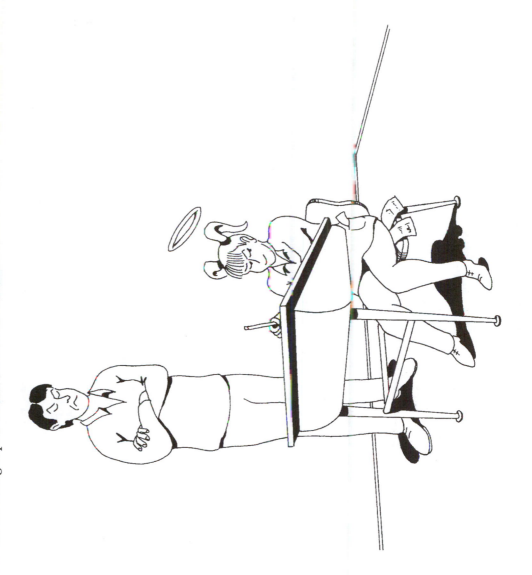

103

4. Erase your notes from the chalkboard.

5. Have the students sit where they cannot see each other's work.

6. Separate friends.

7. Do not allow students to wear jackets or other bulky clothing during a test.

8. Lock up or guard your tests and answer sheets.

9. Change your test somewhat—or even totally—for a rewrite.

10. When a row of students sits beside the chalkboard, remove all the brushes. This prevents a note's being put under a chalk brush and slid up and down the chalk rail.

11. Ensure that one copy of your test does not circulate after one class has written it. Number them if you teach the same subject in more than one class.

12. Make new tests each year, so copies of your old tests do not float from sibling or friend to sibling or friend.

13. Do not throw old copies of your tests in the trash can while students are in the room.

14. Have students bring a novel (to be placed on the floor) for when they have finished a test. It will give students something silent to do after the quiz and will therefore reduce the temptation to help others. You can also provide word puzzles at this point.

15. Survey desk tops to see if answers have been written on them.

16. The best environment for preventing cheating is at desks placed strategically apart in the school gym, with many supervisors looking on.

17. Watch for a student who is continually watching you.

18. Keep an eye and an ear out for the cough, sneeze, or clear-the-throat signal system. With true-and-false tests, the leader, usually a better student, will sneeze or clear his or her throat for true and cough for false. This is done semiquietly, so you will not notice.

19. Watch for the Morse Code cheating trick. This sometimes occurs between students who have access to the code by way of military or other training. The students doing this will be nonchalantly tapping their pens on their desks or papers: —·—·.

20. Do not allow students to open their desks.

21. Walk up and down the rows while wearing soft-soled shoes.

22. Do not allow students to use a pencil sharpener during tests.

23. Keep an eye out for hand signals, especially among peers.

24. Do not allow students to lend equipment (pens, pencils, erasers, etc.) during tests.

25. Look at students' shoes and socks to see if slips of paper are sticking out.

26. Look for watch calculators during math tests.

27. Do not allow pencil cases or tissue boxes to be on a student's desk during a quiz or test.

104

28. Watch the person who drops a pen or pencil during a test. This may be an attempt to lean over for a better look at a neighbor's test paper.

29. Watch for any open books on the floor.

30. Keep an eye out for any student writing abnormally large answers so his or her friends can see them.

31. Do not allow students to leave their desks to ask you clarification questions; have them put their hands up and you go to them. If a student comes to your desk, this obstructs your view and gives the student an opportunity to survey others' work.

32. Watch for passing papers.

33. Don't leave the room during a test—especially for a student visitor at your classroom door with a "crisis." It may be a setup to get you out for a couple of seconds.

34. Watch for notebooks being pulled out of desks.

35. Watch for a well-written-on eraser.

36. Have zero tolerance for talking during tests.

37. If you suspect a student, check his or her arms and hands for answers written on them.

38. Do not allow unrelated texts or notebooks to be on students' desks.

39. Check pen casings; some students will write answers on rolled-up paper in thick pens that can be taken apart.

40. If your situation warrants or allows it, have a teacher aide or school official help supervise a test.

Guidelines to Discourage Cheating on Assignments

41. Make sure handwriting on a report or essay is consistent in style and form.

42. Have students turn in handwritten rough copies of work that is typed. This allows you to at least know the student has covered the data.

43. Watch for the purchased or Internet essay or report. If you suspect this, photocopy it. You may get it a second time from another student.

44. Do not have the same report or essay topics from year to year. This keeps students from copying them from an older brother or sister.

Guidelines to Discourage Cheating As a Result of Marking

45. When marking, put an "X" directly on the wrong answer, not beside it.

46. Mark a double "XX" on all blank answer spaces, so students cannot fill them in later and say *you* made a mistake. If you put only one X, students can write in the correct answer beside your X. Two X's mean it was blank.

47. Check for the same wrong answers between students who sat close to each other.

48. It is best not to have an exchange of test papers for speedy marking, as prior arrangements to mark wrong answers correct may have been made among friends.

SPECIAL CIRCUMSTANCES

49. Have the much-requested open-book test. This will eliminate most of the circumstances necessary for cheating. (Remember, open-book tests are often more difficult because a thorough knowledge of the text is required.)

50. In certain circumstances and with certain classes, it may be wise not to use the names "test" or "quiz" as such for your evaluation tools. With some classes (e.g., English), it is possible to make a test look like a regular assignment, or it may be possible to grade a regular assignment and use this as your evaluation tool. In this case, the evaluation should be called a "process evaluation." If you do not have tests per se, you can, in fact, reduce cheating. Many students tighten up when they are writing a test and cheat because they feel unable to write the "monster" before them. The process evaluation will eliminate anxieties and fears associated with tests because this type of evaluation is not different from the norm or routine of the classroom.

106

Section Two

PROBLEM-SOLVING MANAGEMENT TECHNIQUES THAT KEEP STUDENTS ON TASK

Every student in every classroom must work in order to ensure success. We all know that when students are on task there are few, if any, behavior problems. The hard-working classroom is a pleasure for everybody; the students benefit from what they learn, and you benefit from reduction in stress.

This second section gives you sound, reliable ideas to help keep students willingly on task, working hard, and enjoying the learning process.

51

THE JOB JAR AND FIFTY JOBS

When teachers present a regular lesson and have an assignment associated with that lesson, some students will be very skillful and finish early. Idle students will begin to talk and interfere with others still on task. Some may even become physically abusive at this time. It is important, therefore, to have a time-filler technique or idea that you can put into action instantly when the need arises. The student Job Jar truly solves the extra time problem.

How It Works

1. Photocopy and cut out the list of fifty job-jar jobs and place them in a large unbreakable jar.

2. When a student is finished work early, have him or her draw a job from the jar. Once the student has read the task, he or she is to replace the idea in the jar.

3. These jobs are all designed to have some educational value. Each one can be worked on at the student's desk and doesn't require special materials that are not normally available in a classroom.

4. The evaluation of the results of work from the job jar is at your discretion.

The Fifty Job-Jar Jobs

1. Write a one-page argument on why people should or should not have to do work drawn from job jars.

2. Using the encyclopedia, find someone who has written a book. Describe this person in three sentences.

3. Describe an invention in three sentences.

4. Put your classmates' names in alphabetical order.

5. Make a list of 27 things in the classroom and put them in alphabetical order.

6. Take a full page from a storybook; find all the words that begin with "a" and "b." Put these words in alphabetical order.

7. Choose any page of the dictionary; write out only those words with two syllables.

8. Find ten of the longest or most unusual words in the last story you read. Find what they mean in the dictionary. Write a good sentence using each word.

9. Write out the bibliography of the three books closest to you or three of the ones you like.

10. Get a copy of the newspaper. Read the first three pages.

11. Go to the encyclopedia, find the name of a musician or composer, and write five sentences describing this person.

12. Read the letters to the editor of your local paper. Describe the best letter in three sentences.

13. Describe what you want to do or to be when you finally finish school.

14. Write a short paragraph describing your neighborhood.

15. Add up the ages of all the people you know the age of or add the ages of all your family members in months, hours, minutes, seconds.

16. Draw a picture of the main character in the last book you read. Put lines extending out all around him or her. Describe that person with one word at the end of those lines.

17. List the words of the last story you read that help you see, smell, or hear things the author is talking about.

18. Describe what an elephant looks like.

19. Compare an elephant to a dump truck.

20. Describe a Saturday morning cartoon show. Tell why you like or dislike certain characters.

21. Read a biography (a story written about a person's life). Write four sentences that tell of important events in the life of the person.

22. Read a made-up or fictional story.

23. Write out the alphabet from memory. Write out the times tables from memory.

24. Write the alphabet in reverse.

25. List the titles of as many of the books you have read as possible.

26. Draw and color a picture of some object in the classroom, but put it in a different setting or background.

27. In three sentences, describe how the setting of the last story you read is different from your neighborhood.

28. Draw and color something to eat, for example, candy bar, piece of pie, potatoes. Label the drawing (what it is) and describe how it is eaten.

29. Draw and color a picture of the most important part of the last story you read.

30. Memorize or write a poem; be sure to use the proper punctuation.

31. Make a time line to fit a story. Start with what happened at the beginning and list things in order after that.

32. Draw a map of the last story you read or draw a map of your area. Label this map. Remember to print on the map.

33. In all the stories and books you have read, what was the best setting or location? Describe this in five good sentences.

110

34. Use the encyclopedia to find a former president who is not well known. Describe the best thing about this person.

35. Make a word-find puzzle using the names of the teachers in the school.

36. Draw and color a picture of what happened in a cartoon show.

37. Draw and color a picture of something fun that happened in school this week or last week.

38. Make a cartoon strip (stick people) to show the most important things that happened in the last story you read or what happened after school yesterday.

39. Tell how the last story you read ended.

40. List all the story and television characters you like and do not like; draw one of them.

41. Read a brand-new story.

42. Write five good sentences that tell the most exciting things that happened yesterday or last week.

43. What is your favorite animal? Describe it in five good sentences.

44. It has been said that everybody has a story about a chicken, a dog, or a cat. If you have one, write out the story.

45. Read about machines, then answer these questions:
a. How do they make life and work easier?
b. How do they help with recreation or leisure time?

46. Go to the encyclopedia and find Philadelphia. Read until you come to the name of two bridges. Write the name of the one that is related to a poet.

47. They say a picture is worth a thousand words. Why do people say this? Find a picture and describe it.

48. Write the words from this week's spelling lesson in alphabetical order.

49. Choose a story character you would like to have in the classroom with you. Tell why in five good sentences.

50. Go to the encyclopedia and read about Abraham Lincoln. List three good things about him. Draw his picture.

The majority of schools from the primary grades on up have a track and field day or sports day at the school that supports the physical education program. On this day, the normal academic routine gives way to a focus on the physical activities or skills of the students.

Track and Field Day has a special importance in terms of physical fitness and the development of self-worth among the participants. The logistics, however, of planning and carrying out the actual events of the day can be a problem—because you must run two types of events, usually simultaneously, if you are going to complete all events in one school day.

The first type—the track events, such as the 100-meter or 400-meter run—are usually separated into heats and then into finals. The second type are field events, such as triple-jump and shot-put. The problem comes when you have to run these two different types of events at the same time and some of the same students may be participating in both types of events.

The secret to success lies in the scheduling and assigning of workers. The following basic rules will help you run your program. These rules are based on a school population of 400 or fewer, but can easily be adapted to suit your situation.

1. Track events must take precedence over field events. Students should be told that if they have a track event and a field event at the same time, they are to report to the track event first.

2. Your workers at the field events must be efficient in terms of time-management skills. They will be required to keep students participating at a reasonable pace and to adjust for any students coming from participating in a track event to do a field event.

3. A concession stand that supports school events or a charitable cause should be run by responsible adults or a strong student who cannot be manipulated.

4. Every student or every second student should have a copy of the day's event schedule, or a large poster of the schedule should be displayed at the center control booth as well as at strategic spots around the event's location.

5. Students should be told which radio station to listen to the morning of the track and field day in case of cancellation due to weather.

6. Ribbons should be given out for first, second, third, and fourth places.

7. A student who has won an event (e.g., shot-put) will take the data to the control booth and pick up his or her ribbon. The first-place winner should be accompanied by second-, third-, and fourth-place winners to ensure that each one gets the proper color of ribbon.

8. If you desire, points can be attached to each win, second place, and so on, so a total points tally for Best Athlete or Best Group of Athletes (e.g., house or class) can be established.

9. A sufficient number of megaphones and other communication devices should be in place and working properly.

10. A staff-versus-students relay is always a good spirit builder as the day winds down.

11. Garbage cleanup must be done before the final event of the day or before awards are given out at the end.

12. Attendance should be taken at the start of the day, after lunch, and at the end of the day.

The Track and Field Meet Schedule (Figure 2-1) gives you an idea of how the actual events run when both track events and field events are running simultaneously. Use the following guidelines:

➧ Each student is participating in a minimum of four events.

➧ Students travel from event to event with peers of a similar age.

➧ This schedule features six age groupings of boys and girls, the times the events occur, and the actual events each group participates in.

➧ This schedule is designed for the track and field meet that is held at one location.

➧ The totality of the track and field events is accommodated in a timed sequence.

➧ The track schedule runs independently of the field events.

➧ Participants in the track events are to proceed as quickly as possible after their track event is finished to the field events they are participating in.

Figure 2-1
TRACK AND FIELD MEET SCHEDULE

FIELD SCHEDULE

TIME	12-13 Boys	14 Boys	15 Boys	12-13 Girls	14 Girls	15 Girls
9:00	L. Jump	H. Jump	T. Jump	———	Javel	Discus
9:45	Shot	Discus	Javel	H. Jump	———	T. Jump
10:30	H. Jump	T. Jump	Discus	Shot	L. Jump	Javel
11:15	Discus	Javel	Shot	T. Jump	H. Jump	L. Jump
12:00	T. Jump	———	L. Jump	Discus	Shot	H. Jump
12:45	Javel	Shot	———	L. Jump	T. Jump	———
1:30	———	L. Jump	H. Jump	Javel	Discus	Shot

TRACK SCHEDULE

TIME	12-13 Boys	14 Boys	15 Boys	12-13 Girls	14 Girls	15 Girls
9:10	100 Meter Heats					
9:20	———	———	Heat	———	———	———
9:40	———	Heat	———	———	———	Heat
10:20	———	———	———	———	Heat	———
11:00	———	———	———	Heat	———	———
11:20	Heat	———	———	———	———	———
12:00	800 Meter Final >>>>>>>>>>>>>>>>>>>>>>>>
12:30	400 Meter Final >>>>>>>>>>>>>>>>>>>>>>>>
1:00	200 Meter Final >>>>>>>>>>>>>>>>>>>>>>>>
1:00	1500 Meter Final >>>>>>>>>>>>>>>>>>>>>>>>
1:30	100 Meter Final >>>>>>>>>>>>>>>>>>>>>>>>
2:00	Relays >>>>>>>>>>>>>>>>>>>>>>>>
2:30						

53 THE NAME GAME—A MEMORY ENHANCER

Teachers need those quick, useful ideas that keep everyone on task, focused to the *nth* degree and—above all—interested and involved. This word memory game can be used as a method of teaching everyone each person's name the first day of school, or it can be used as a vocabulary reinforcer for a subject area.

How It Works

When you use this idea to teach everyone the names of the students in the class, you must start with the student at the front of the first row. You tell the first student that in order to play the game, he or she must tell the class his or her name. She states her name, "Mary Jones," for example; the next student in the row says his or her name, after repeating the name of the first person. If the second person's name is Keisha Smith, then Keisha says, "Mary Jones, Keisha Smith." The third person named Edward Wu says, "Mary Jones, Keisha Smith, Edward Wu," and so on. It taxes the students' ability when the number of names is more than ten. Some will forget a few, but it will amaze you how many can repeat all the names of the twenty-eight or so students you have in the class.

This is a wonderful exercise for you to take part in, also. It will certainly improve your memory of the names. If you take part, leave yourself for last and repeat all the names with yours at the end. Actually, it will be easier for you because you have the class list to study ahead of time.

This idea can be expanded to reinforce the vocabulary of a subject area. If you are studying cities in countries of the world, for example, the first student says, "New York, U.S.A."; the second student responds by saying, "New York, U.S.A.; Nairobi, Kenya." The third then repeats, "New York, U.S.A.; Nairobi, Kenya," and adds another city in another country of the world—"Beijing, China," for example; and so on, until the last person tries to remember twenty-eight or thirty cities and their countries, depending on how many students you have in the class.

This is an excellent memory enhancer and adds a great deal of fun to the learning process. It really holds the attention of the students; no one will be off task.

SANDPAPER LETTERS

If you are a kindergarten or grade 1 teacher, you have to be, by the very nature of the job, a hard-working, dedicated person. It is your mandate to get children started on the education road. Like all of us, you need resources and techniques to help you with that major task.

Kindergarten and grade 1 teachers must introduce the basics of letter and number formations or shapes. The unique idea given here will effectively help you introduce these concepts to your group of hands-on children. With this concept, you make letter and number shapes that have a texture, so students can use their tactile sense to aid in the learning process.

WHAT TO DO

1. Cut number and letter shapes out of sandpaper and glue these onto a stiff card-board backing that is the shape of the letter or number.

2. It's wise to use different grits of sandpaper for differing needs; for example, the lower-case letters can be made from 50- to 100-grit sandpaper, and upper-case letters from 100- to 150-grit; numbers can be made from 150- to 200-grit. Make vowels out of very fine sandpaper of 220 grit or more.

3. The letters and numbers must be a minimum of 3 inches (77 mm) high, with the stems of the letters not less than 3/4 inch (20 mm) wide. The upper-case letters should be a minimum of 1/2 inch (15 mm) larger than the lower-case letters.

4. For a variation of this idea, use pieces of rug or different textures of material to make the letters. In that case, you could make all the letters one color or pattern and all the numbers another color, and so forth.

5. The sandpaper letters are excellent for assisting students who print certain letters or numbers in reverse. Not only does it give the visual aid of seeing the letters, but the tactile action helps the child to internalize the proper shape of the letters.

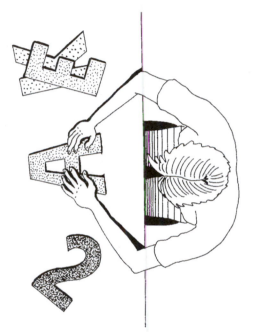

116

54

LEVEL GROUPING FOR MAXIMUM LEARNING

Every classroom has a variety of skill levels of students. You may have a group of budding molecular physicists in your classroom, along with students who are at the low end of the scale in skills. This causes a problem for you; you want to present the required curriculum to all in an equal, yet individualized, way to draw out the greatest potential of each student, because all students are equal and all are persons of worth.

The question is, how can you stimulate the Einsteins in your class, yet at the same time develop the curriculum knowledge in the average and slower students who will require more repetition of the information?

To help answer this question, the following grouping technique can be utilized.

➤ Place students in groups within your classroom according to their academic ability level.

➤ Have the students arrange their desks in a circle, so they face each other.

➤ Place an empty desk in the circle for you. This desk should be strategically located in each group, so that when you sit in it, you will be able to see the other students in their groups.

➤ Instruct all students in all groups to listen to you as you make the first presentation.

➤ Present the required curriculum data to the top-end students first as you sit in their circle. Speak loudly enough for the students in the other groups to hear your explanation. When you have finished presenting the information to the upper-level students, it may be worthwhile to present this group with an assignment that requires a higher level of expertise than that required for the other groups. Depending on the skills of this first group, they may not need to listen to what is said at the other groups as you move along.

➤ You then proceed to group 2, which is at the second level of ability. While you sit with this group, you tell groups 3, 4, and so on, to continue to listen. Then repeat the lesson you gave to the first group. Remember to speak loudly enough for the remaining groups to hear your instruction. Present this group with the regular assignment.

➤ When you have finished instructing group 2, move along to the empty desk at the next lowest ability group and present the same lesson to the students. By the time you finish with this third group, they will have heard the data presented three times. Depending on how many groups you have, the final set of students could have heard the curriculum data seven or eight times. Repetition reinforces the learning of material. This is especially important for students with fewer academic skills.

➤ If a student in group 2 needs to reconsider a point or two, he or she simply listens to your presentation to group 3 or 4.

This concept of level grouping will help maintain classroom control as you teach. Students in the group you are in will, of course, be focused on your teaching. The other groups will be in your field of vision and will either be listening to you or working on a regular or enriched assignment.

THE CLASS PARTS MANAGER

Many students do not come to class prepared; they do not bring pens, pencils, or texts. For some, it is a genuine case of forgetfulness, but for others, it is a game; they know they will have to go back to their lockers to fetch the proper equipment. This causes you four sets of problems:

1. The student who is out fetching a pen will disrupt the proceedings when she or he returns.

2. You will have to reteach a concept or two for the student who was out of the classroom.

3. You have no guarantee that the student will return with the proper materials—or even return at all to the classroom. She or he may skip out.

4. If you lend the necessary pens, pencils, or other materials to the student, there is a strong likelihood that you will not get the equipment back. This is especially true if there is a degree of hustle and bustle at the end of a class.

How to Minimize the Problem

Appoint a Class Parts Manager for your supply of pens, pencils, protractors, and other regularly needed materials. It is this Parts Manager's responsibility to control the flow of equipment to students who do not bring the proper materials to class.

118

With this setup, the student without equipment is not allowed to go out of the room to his or her locker for the proper materials. The Parts Manager lends her or him the necessary materials, and the student receiving them has to sign for them.

When class is finished, the Parts Manager automatically gathers the equipment and marks whether it was returned on the Materials Lent Out form (Figure 2-2). The Materials Lent Out form has an added feature that will help in retrieving materials if the student should slip away without returning them; the borrowing student must indicate the location of her or his next class. If a student gets away with a pen, you simply send a note to the other teacher to tell the student to give your materials back to the person who brought the note.

The Materials Lent Out form will help you in one other way; by using the form, you now have a record of which students are frequent offenders in the no pen, no pencil, and so on, department. This information can be useful when it comes to parent-teacher conference time.

Figure 2-2
MATERIALS LENT OUT

Name: _____ Date: _____

Materials lent out. _____

What is the location of the class you will have after this class? _____

I promise to return all materials lent to me. I understand that the teacher may contact my parent or guardian in order to retrieve materials.

_____
Student Signature

57

TIMER CONTROLS

Students must be kept on task. This is not always easy to do when you have a group working independently at a work station, and you are working with a different group on the other side of the class. You need an effective way to keep the first group on task for a certain period of time; you need a "work-time framer."

If, for example, you want that group in the corner to work on number facts or algebra skills for a solid fifteen minutes, how do you create that exact block of time so students do not shut down, quit early, or go on to some other task before the end of the allotted time?

One idea that works well in this situation is to use an inexpensive kitchen timer, which will ring after a specific period of time has passed. When the timer is set, students are to be told that they must be working on the assigned task until the timer rings. You will see that students will work to the timer and pace themselves accordingly. The kitchen timer idea is successful because it is clear and precise—the way students like to have things defined.

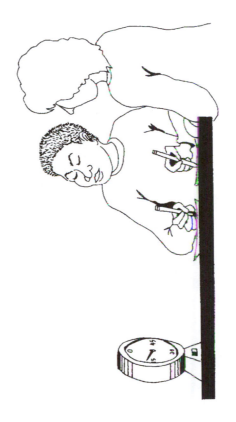

THE TWELVE BIG DON'TS OF TEACHING

When you have a few years in the modern classroom, you begin to realize that when dealing with the variabilities of students, parents, and staff, there are some things you should not do. These lessons are sometimes learned the hard way over the years, and it is best to store these "don'ts" carefully in your memory for instant recall.

THE DON'TS

1. Don't lie. Students can spot this in you, and then everything you say will lack credibility.

2. Don't compare one student with another. Don't compare boys with girls. Don't compare siblings.

3. Don't do something you do not want your students to do; for example, if you make a paper airplane and throw it in the class (even if it is not pointy), one of your students will make a pointy paper airplane and hit someone smack-dab in the eye (worst-case scenarios *do* happen).

4. Don't say, "I don't care."

5. Don't get into a conflict. Avoid a confrontation at all costs; remove yourself or the student, if possible, until things calm down.

6. Don't swear or curse in the classroom.

7. Don't try to please or appease the constantly bitter staff member; it does not work.

8. Don't run videos or take students to movies without having previewed them for language and suitability of content.

9. Don't run videos or photocopy material without consideration of copyright or school board policies.

10. Don't be swayed by the demands or requests of parents to teach something they want, if it deviates from the curriculum. Tell them they must get approval from the school board first.

11. Don't put down students' physical, social, emotional, family, or economic situations.

12. Don't debate classroom management issues with a class of students; you always end up with a teacher-versus-students battle. No matter how much a student supports you on an issue, when talking one to one, that same student will not disagree with his or her peers in the class.

122

SHARED WRITING

In the early or primary grades, it is important to keep students attentive at all times. Because they are younger, it is not always easy to make sure all students are paying attention. You need methods of focusing the children on the task of learning the basics, such as number facts and English skills.

One of the best ways to maintain student concentration while working in the basic skill areas is to use the "shared writing" idea. Shared writing is the creation of a letter or message in view of all of the students. It normally would include the date, the weather, and any announcements. Unique to this idea is that it also highlights or spotlights one of the students in the class.

How It Works

1. Shared writing is usually presented in the first period of school in the morning or immediately after lunch in the afternoon.

2. Once students have entered the classroom, they are all to sit in a semicircle around a large notepad or chart paper on an easel.

3. You then pick the student to be spotlighted (usually on a rotating basis). You introduce this person and use his or her name as part of the lesson.

123

4. The featured student now gets a chance to share with you and the class something he or she wants to put into the message. This may be how old he or she is, where he or she lives, and so forth. You write this information in a positive way. (e.g., "Jackie is five beautiful years old.")

5. Print the message, with each sentence being a different color (use markers).

6. With shared writing, you are able to focus attention on all the elements needed in basic English skills. Some of the areas that attention can be directed to are:

➠ Spelling
➠ Phonics
➠ Punctuation
➠ Writing dates
➠ Capitalization
➠ Letter shapes
➠ Repetition of letters
➠ Number-to-word relationships
➠ Neatness

7. The highlighted student of the day is then allowed to take the large colorful shared letter home. The child is asked to read and explain it to his or her parents. Most parents will pick up on this and make it a focal point for family discussion that day.

The beauty of shared writing is that it is a high attention enhancer, as well as a self-esteem builder. All students enjoy hearing information about themselves and about their friends. The student focused upon has gained "warm fuzzies" from a positive presentation of his or her information—and you have taught the basics of the English language.

124

60

THE DESK PAK STORAGE PROBLEM SOLVER

Solving problems in the classroom requires you to be very creative and resourceful. One area that definitely needs a little creativity thrown its way is the problem of storage. Storage space in the classroom must be continuously accessible, be user-friendly, and not involve a great deal of noise when used.

Perhaps one of the most inventive classroom ideas that meets the above criteria is the Desk Pak Storage System. The Desk Pak (see diagram for dimensions) is a handmade, extra-storage sleeve with pockets that fits over the back of a student's desk chair.

SOME ADVANTAGES AND USES OF THE DESK PAK SYSTEM

1. This storage system provides an excellent location for reading books and other larger items.

2. A deluxe model can be made with zippered or snapped pockets that would allow for the storage of smaller items, such as pens and pencils.

3. The Desk Pak can be made from an old pair of blue jeans, thus reducing the cost.

4. This storage system can travel with the student from grade to grade, usually retiring after grade 7. The Desk Pak will give students some discipline over the organization of books, papers, and notebooks as they go through their day-to-day activities.

5. It works well behind a teacher's desk chair, too! And this great idea can be modified for your own home use. It can store computer disks, sewing supplies, hobby materials, and so forth.

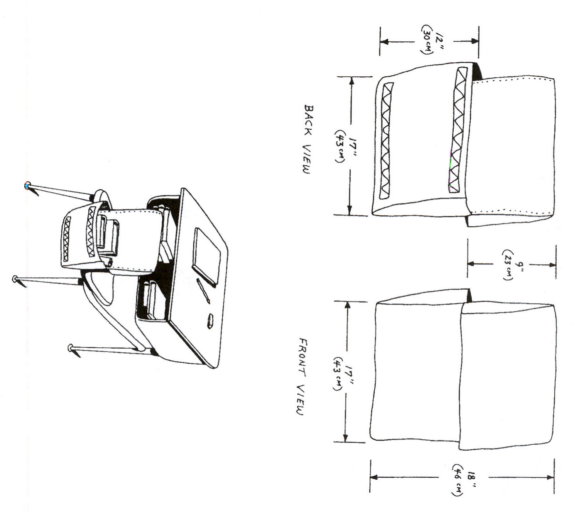

BACK VIEW

12"
(30 cm)

17"
(43 cm)

9"
(23 cm)

FRONT VIEW

17"
(43 cm)

18"
(46 cm)

126

61

STUMP THE EXPERTS

Unique ideas that focus the attention of the students on task—and in the process are a great deal of fun—are a true rarity. The panel game "Stump the Experts" fits this description perfectly. This game will reinforce the learning of your curriculum material like no other, and—what's more—it costs nothing and requires no preparation on your part.

For this game to function, you must have worked in a unit of study for some time; you must feel that the students have a strong general knowledge of the topic. Such subjects as science, geology, history, and civics are ideal for this game.

How It Works

1. Ask all the students in the class to prepare at least three serious written questions on the subject area. Tell the students they will be presenting these to a panel of experts.

2. You next select three students from the class to act as your panel of experts.

3. The class is then allowed in turn to try to stump this panel of experts with their questions.

4. If the person asking the question is able to stump the panel of expert students, then that person must answer it himself or herself. If a student is able to properly answer his or her own question, you then can do one of two things as a reward. You can give the person who stumped the panel 500 points to build toward a prize, or you can replace one of the panel members with the person who stumped them.

5. Once the experts have had their quota of questions (at your discretion), it is a good idea to switch the three on the panel with a fresh set of three experts from the student audience.

The Four Big Pluses of "Stump the Experts"

1. This is a wonderfully effective way to reinforce subject matter at the end of a unit or before a test.

2. All students will focus on the game; therefore, classroom management is no problem.

3. Students get a chance to show off their questioning and knowledge skills.

4. This taps into the natural competitiveness of students. The questions will be difficult and the responses will amaze you.

128

THE OLD-FASHIONED SPELLING BEE

Some teaching techniques are older than the grandparents of Methuselah, yet are still going strong because they work. They are effective teaching tools that reinforce the learning of materials. The old-fashioned spelling bee is one of these beauties, and here is how it works.

Divide the class into two groups of about the same ability level. Have group 1 stand in a line on one side of the classroom and group 2 on the other side.

You then proceed to ask the first student in row 1 to spell a word (usually from the week's spelling list). If he or she gets it right, that person can remain standing in line. If, however, a student does not spell the word correctly, he or she must sit down at his or her desk.

The asking of words to spell passes from one group to the other with each new word. You may ask a person from the other group to spell a word that was missed by the first group you asked, or you may use a different word from your spelling list for the next member of the other group. The spelling of words alternates between the two groups until one side is left standing with one or more members, and there is no one left in the other group. The side with the persons remaining is the winner.

The old-fashioned spelling bee is a busy activity for the students; they are attentive to task and usually are not behavior problems during the process of the bee. In addition, this old-fashioned spelling bee is a wonderful reinforcer of spelling skills. You will find students thinking before they blurt out an answer. It is the thinking about how to spell words that makes students truly internalize the lesson.

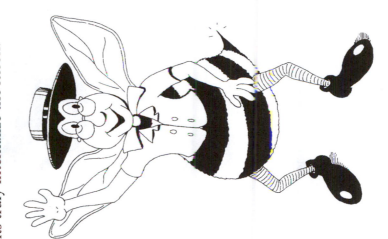

Buzz...B-u-z-z

129

THE NEW-FASHIONED SPELLING BEE

At no other time in world history have literary skills been so important. High on the scale of importance is the ability to spell properly. Spelling skills are seen by educators and employers as fundamental to communication in this modern technological society. Indeed, proficiency in all literary skill areas is sought as students leave institutions of learning.

To reinforce fundamental spelling skills, you need a technique that will keep the students' interest while enhancing spelling proficiency. The new-fashioned spelling bee is the answer.

How It Works

1. Separate the students into two groups—Team A and Team B. Give each team a box that has five copies of all the letters of the alphabet. These letters should be approximately two to five inches high and be made from stiff, durable cardboard. (Students can make these ahead of time.)

2. Once each team has a complete box of letters, place Team A on one side of the classroom and Team B on the other side.

3. Place a desk or table in front of each team and tell them to set their box on it.

130

4. You then stand far enough back so you can see both teams of students at one time.

5. Start the game by reading one of the words from the spelling list. The teams are to scramble into their boxes in order to come up with the correct letters to spell the word. Each different letter of the word must be held up by a different person as the students line up, spelling the word. The team that spells the word correctly first is the winner of that round. The team that wins the greatest number of rounds (words spelled) is the overall winner.

6. You will notice that you will not need all the students in the team to spell the word every time, so part of the game is for the students to have quality decision-making skills on how to organize within a group. They must decide which students of their group are to spell the word each time in the most efficient manner.

THE BEST BOOK REPORT FORM
IN THE BUSINESS

Every teacher needs those day-to-day problem solvers that require a minimum of prep time and yet provide a quality learning experience for the students. The Book Report Form (Figure 2-3) fits this situation to a "T." This form is designed to draw out of the student the maximum amount of information about any novel or story he or she has read. The form was created to be as universal and stimulating as possible. No longer will students say, "We don't know what to write about," because topic areas are furnished.

How It Works

1. This book report form must be presented to the students just prior to reading any required book. When the book report form is first presented, provide the students with a thorough explanation of each question. This will clear up any uncertainties.

2. There are two things to fill in on the book report form before you photocopy it for your students. These are the number of pages you require for the report (in item 2) and the number of characters you want described in the character sketch (in item 5).

3. You will notice that this form requires logical written answers. There are no "fill-in-the-blank" spaces requiring one-word responses. This allows for ideas to be more fully developed or explained.

4. The form itself causes students to consider the essentials of plot, characterization, setting, and theme, which are central to an in-depth understanding of any book or novel.

5. One of the nice things about this book report form is the fact that it can be used throughout the year for any number of books you require in your English, literature, or languages program.

Figure 2-3
THE BOOK REPORT FORM

1. Provide a bibliographical description of the book as follows: Author's Name, Title of the Book, Place of Publication, Publisher, Date Published.

2. This book report would be a minimum of _____ full pages in length.

3. The setting is where the action of the book takes place. Describe the setting(s) of the book.

4. Each book has a theme, for example, Good vs. Evil. What was the theme of your book?

5. A character sketch is a description of a person or persons in the book. Provide a character sketch of _____ "character(s)." You must give us as total a picture as possible of the individual you are describing. You must make this person "come alive" for the teacher. Use the outline provided.

6. Each book has words that either are new to you or are interesting. List ten of these with their directory definitions.

7. Choose a paragraph in the book that you feel sums up the story or that you thought was interesting and write it in the report.

8. What part of the book affected you the most? Describe.

9. As you read this book, you formed an opinion about it. You either enjoyed it, you were mediocre (so-so) about it, or you disliked it. Please describe how you feel about this book.

CHARACTER SKETCH OUTLINE

1. Describe the person physically, for example, age, height, weight, size, hair color, shoe size, handicaps, body language, distinctive features (warts, pimples, limps, etc.).

2. Outline the person's mental attitude, for example, happy, sad, manic, bitter, deranged, critical, mean, joyous, altruistic (happy), self pitying.

3. What was the history or the background of the person like—poor, abused, spoiled, over-worked, middle class, rich?

4. How did the character change through the circumstances of the book?

65 THE MONTHLY SEATING PLAN ROTATION SYSTEM

Some ideas that promote classroom management are simple, and yet extremely effective, in terms of problem solving. At the same time, those concepts promote an aspect of learning that in the long term is important for students to have internalized. The monthly seating plan rotation system does this.

The problem solved by this is the criticism sometimes leveled at teachers that a student has been placed beside someone he or she does not get along with, and therefore his or life is now miserable. The monthly seating plan rotation system will destroy this criticism forever and, at the same time, teach students they must learn to tolerate even those they do not get along with.

What to Do

1. Cut the students' names off the class list or nominal roll and place them as individual name tags in a draw box to be used once a month. At the start of each month, have the students come up to the draw box in random order to pick a name out of the box. The name of the person a student draws will be the name of the person who sits at the desk or location where he or she is sitting now.

   A second way to facilitate this rotation is to number each desk or location and have students themselves come up to the draw box and choose a location or desk number indicating where they will sit for a month. In effect, with either of these two draw systems, the teacher is not the decision maker as to who sits where; it is purely the luck of the draw.

2. When the students' new placements are drawn for each month, there should be no choice about moving to that desk or location. Students must learn to make adjustments and be flexible with whatever neighbor they have. This message should be taught as part of a lesson on tolerance prior to the first draw for desks or locations.

3. Provision must be made for special cases, for example, students who have vision or hearing problems, when assigning desks or locations to the students.

Advantages

1. Gone is the criticism that you placed little Johnny or Maria permanently in a location or desk that was intolerable. You neither placed the student there, nor is the posting permanent.

2. If all efforts fail and a student simply cannot "survive" in the location he or she is in, that student must still wait a month to have the environment change.

3. The buzzword or expression for the latter half of the twentieth century was IQ, but employers, social workers, and counselors of all sorts are now saying *interactive compatibility*—getting along while working together. By having the students learn to tolerate new people in their neighborhood space in the classroom, you are promoting interactive compatibility, and thus developing a skill in the students that will be of value for the rest of their lives.

134

THE INSTANT NEWSPAPER ASSIGNMENT

Teachers are always looking for ways to keep students working on tasks with high interest or highly motivating ideas. The problem to be solved is, where do you find a truly educational assignment that requires little, if any, preparation—one that will be inspiring enough to keep the students' "noses to the grindstone" from beginning to end? The Instant Newspaper Assignment solves this problem.

How It Works

1. To do this assignment, students are to find items in the newspaper. They then cut out and glue the items on a large board or in their notebooks.

2. This newspaper assignment requires very little preparation on your part. You must provide each student or group of students with a photocopy of the Instant Newspaper Assignment Form (Figure 2-4). You must also give each student or group of students a copy of the daily newspaper.

3. The Instant Newspaper Assignment is a wonderful current events and contents locating tool. It forces students to search most areas of the paper. Many students do not read the newspaper to any extent. As a result, they do not know where to find the things they need or want when they do pick up a newspaper. The twenty items to find cause a student to look on almost every page of the average daily newspaper, including two indexes that further help students to locate items.

4. This newspaper assignment can be used as a "starter" assignment for larger newspaper programs that are available from many daily newspapers. Quite a few newspapers have prepared excellent materials for school use. One phone call will net you a plethora of information and materials. Some newspapers even have "educational representatives" who are more than willing to come to your classroom to introduce a program or talk to your students.

135

Figure 2-4

THE INSTANT NEWSPAPER ASSIGNMENT FORM

FIND THESE:

The index that tells where things are in the paper	The classified ad index	An ad for a car or motorcycle	A movie ad
Two ads to come to church	A story, article, or picture about the environment or wildlife	The name of the newspaper	A picture of some sports action or the name of a sports team
An advice column	A "Business Opportunity" classified ad	Three "Help Wanted" ads—1 big, 2 small	A front-page news item
A cartoon	The weather description or forecast	A TV listing	A crossword puzzle or information on a recreational activity; for example, bridge game
An article or story from a foreign country	An obituary listing—sometimes these are listed under "Announcements" or "Deaths"	An editorial	An ad for a food product

67   THE WHO, WHAT, WHEN, WHERE, WHY, AND HOW OF IT ALL—A LESSON IN CONTINUITY

Here is a terrific attention grabber and problem solver for an English, Spanish, French, or other language class where you plan to teach story-writing skills. The problem is, how can you cause students to focus on the basic elements of a story and see what happens to a story line when the elements are not connected or have little or no continuity?

The following technique will use contrast to show students how much more logical or viable a story is if all the basic elements are used together or considered when developing the story.

HOW TO GET STARTED

1. Give out a photocopy of the Story Elements Sheet (Figure 2-5) to individual groups of six students.

2. With this technique, each person in the group of six will fill in one of the elements of who, what, when, where, why, and how, as they together create a story.

3. The first person starts by filling in the "who" of the story with a character description (no one- or two-word responses allowed). After person 1 has filled in his or her character part, that person hands the story to person 2, who fills in the "what" part, and so on, until all six persons have added their ideas to one of the elements and thus created a story.

But there is a catch:

The next part of this technique requires you to use the above ideas in three distinct forms that, when completed, will lead your students to an understanding of the need for continuity in story construction.

FORM A

Have each individual student write his or her element of the story blind. This means that the person who writes the "who" of the story describes the character he or she creates, then folds the paper over to conceal the part written from the person who writes the next element, or the "what" of the story. In turn, the person writing the "what" of the story folds the paper over again to conceal what he or she has written. Each person is writing an element or part of the story without seeing any other part of the work. Of course, the story that results from this process is very disjointed, and often quite humorous. You can point out to the class that this is the result of an almost total lack of continuity.

FORM B

This is the next step in our quest for continuity in a story. In this form, each student still fills in one of the story elements; however, this time each person writing an element is allowed to read what the single previous person has written. For example, the person writing the "where" part of the story is permitted to read (by unfolding) the "when" part

137

but not the "what" part of the story. The results from this exercise will have more continuity than the exercise in Form A, but there still will not be a logical, progressive plot line.

FORM C

The third pattern or way of writing this assignment is for each student to be able to read what all the previous people have written.

As the story elements list is passed to each successive person, he or she is to write or add to the plot. Each student writes using the information placed in the element spaces by the other student or students in the group. The story that evolves from this third pattern, of course, will have the greatest continuity.

The differences in story sequence or progression will be quite clear from one form to another and will quite dramatically show the students that if a story is to have a coherent plot line, the elements of that story must be taken into consideration in a logical, cohesive package.

138

Figure 2-5
STORY ELEMENTS SHEET

WHO	WHAT	WHEN	WHERE	WHY	HOW

CHARADES—A TERRIFIC TOOL

One of the most challenging realities you will face in teaching is the continuous need to come up with interesting ways to stimulate, encourage, and enrich your students.

It is always wonderful to find a technique that works well and keeps the students on task. The game of charades is the lively way to do this. In effect, you "kill two birds with one stone" with this game. The students internalize the required information, and you keep discipline problems at a minimum because the students are diligently participating.

Charades is an oldie but a goodie. Basically, charades is a guessing game wherein one member of a group stands to give a dramatic wordless, or pantomime, presentation describing a word, phrase, or whole sentence. The person's group then attempts to guess what the presenter is trying to act out.

Using this concept in the classroom is not a great deal different from the way it is used at a party or social gathering. Many students have played charades before, so some of the performances will be excellent.

You will need to target the words and phrases you want to reinforce with this concept. Some events are very dramatic and lend themselves to being enacted quite nicely (e.g., Teddy Roosevelt's charge up San Juan Hill).

Once you have gathered enough ideas, place them in a hat. Call the students up one at a time to draw and act out the historical, social, psychological, or other events they were "lucky" enough to draw.

Depending on the nature of your class, it may be advisable to ask for a volunteer to start. This should be an experienced person who will most often get the game started in a positive, upbeat manner. In any event, it is best not to let students see the topic they are going to act out until the draw. This adds to the spontaneity of the presentation.

Charades is a great idea that just needs to be taken out of the closet, dusted off a little, and put to work.

69 WONDERFULLY UNIQUE IDEAS OF MERIT

As a writer completes research on a manuscript, that very research will take him or her down some rabbit trails and through considerably interesting theories or points of view. The following seven rather different ideas have strength in themselves. These ideas are offered to you now as intellectual morsels for you to contemplate, use, and enjoy.

1. The hidden tape recorder technique. This was used near the end of a lesson on Abraham Lincoln's Gettysburg Address. The teacher was just about to wrap up when she pushed the button on her remote control to activate the playing of this very speech on a tape recorder hidden in the classroom. (Actually, she had it hidden in the ceiling tiles, but you do not have to do this.) It sounded like the real thing, as the tape was made with help from a cooperative colleague.

   The students, startled at first, broke out in broad smiles as they realized what was happening. The Gettysburg Address was learned very well that day by her students.

2. When students enter a classroom, they usually wait for the teacher to begin the proceedings; this is not always so in one class. The teacher quite often has the students' assignments placed in envelopes on the rack under the students' desks (not on top, so early arrivers will not peek at others). When students come into the class, they reach under their desks and open the envelopes.

   Sometimes, everyone has the same assignment, and sometimes all or only some are individualized. In any event, it is always an exciting time as the students' natural curiosity causes them to rush to class to see what awaits them in their envelopes.

   It should be noted that the teacher does this on an irregular basis. Students never know when the envelope will be in place, which leads to sporadic reinforcement. This type of reinforcement is most likely to create continuous interest, and therefore students are likely to be on time for this class.

3. Use some sort of electronic noisemaker if you need to preserve your voice for one reason or another. These noisemakers can be purchased at any toy store and can be quite effective if used correctly and with discretion. If the noisemaker is used excessively to gain attention, the students will soon tune it out.

4. The "family star" is a wonderful PR idea that can be used on certain special holidays—or at any time of the year. Have each family make a fairly large "family star" with all sorts of decorations and pictures on it.

   Each family's star is hung in the school foyer, hallways, offices, or other location where fire regulations allow it. This idea gives a sense of ownership and belonging to the parents, especially, as they enter your school for parent-teacher conferences and special programs. Note here: *Care must be taken not to leave out students from dysfunctional families.* In these cases, you can help the student create a "family star."

5. Teachers are always looking for unique ways to help students internalize what they teach. One unusual way to reinforce the learning of skill areas is to sing the lesson or parts of the lesson to the students. This will highlight certain areas and enrich whole lessons, if you are able to put the math facts to tune.

141

6. Teachers are often called upon to work or direct students in pageants, programs, or stage presentations. One truly creative idea for a stage presentation is to have the students use sign language to make their presentation as it is enacted or is read by a narrator. Your presentation can be performed on stage, with class members using sign language, as it is simultaneously read to the audience. This truly different presentation will have a lasting impact on the audience as well as the students.

142

NUMBER CONTROL

In the ongoing hustle and bustle of the average classroom, teachers must have workable organizational plans or techniques. These concepts must speed up or streamline the ebb and flow of all kinds of data whether it be collecting marks, dealing with student problems, gathering information, or keeping track of student assignments.

One of the best ways to set up that organizational system is to use numbers instead of names. When assigning numbers to the students, do so only up to the number of students in the class. If, for example, you have thirty-seven students, you should assign numbers only up to thirty-seven. You may allow for favorite numbers up to that point, but not beyond, even if Judy insists her favorite number is 47 billion.

SOME ADVANTAGES TO THE NUMBER CONTROL SYSTEM

1. Texts can be assigned by person number; person 14 gets text 14. Everyone then knows who owns or is using what text.

2. Numbers are easily used in sequence, therefore avoiding favoritism for jobs, and other activities.

3. Line-ups are in number sequence, thus avoiding problems with students who are inclined to break into a line. This is especially important when it comes to counting the students after a fire drill or an emergency.

4. If someone (e.g., the librarian) comes to your class to "borrow" a student or two for jobs, ask the borrower to pick a number or two. This is completely objective.

5. Assignments are recorded by number in your filing system. This makes for easier filing because you can collect tests and other work in number order as they occur in your filing cabinet.

6. Numbers are not to be given out by alphabetical order; thus the students with W, X, Y, or Z at the start of their last names will no longer always be last in the order of things.

TWO WAYS TO USE COLORS
TO SOLVE PROBLEMS

In the process of any school day, you need working mechanisms of student behavior control and material management that become indispensable to your teaching program. With the following two ideas for using colors in grouping and organizing, you can maintain order in the classroom and in the logistics of notebooks, binders, and so forth.

IDEA 1

This technique will work best in the primary or elementary grades. Within the first two weeks of school, you will have the class figured out as to which personalities work well together and which ones need to be apart. Divide the class into color groupings of five to seven students. Once grouped, the students will then work within that group for the month, the term, or the year; you determine the amount of time the group is together.

This color grouping has several advantages:

1. You can separate personalities.

2. Work and expectations within the group become predictable for everyone.

3. Every child has a place to belong.

4. Students are to use the color groups for other activities as well, such as which people to sit with while watching television—or for choosing teams in gym or playing games. (This helps to eliminate "left-outs.")

IDEA 2

Gathering student notebooks can get confusing if you have one notebook per subject, and they are all collected together for two or three subjects.

It is therefore a good idea to color-group the notebooks. At the start of the year, have everyone use red notebooks for math, green for science, yellow for English, and so on. If a student cannot get a certain color of notebook for a subject area, a sheet of paper glued to the front of a notebook of another color and colored with a marker will suffice.

This technique is especially useful if you have a pile of notebooks on your desk with, for example, math and English to be corrected. You can instantly see which notebook goes where if things get scattered. Never again will you take home the wrong pile of notebooks to correct!

THE ANIMAL SPELLING CHART

You are looking for a progressive spelling program to apply universally to your class of students whose skill range is quite broad. You need an individualized, yet workable, language arts spelling program that will serve the needs of the lower ability group, yet, at the same time, be of educational worth to the top—end students. The Animal Spelling Chart does this quite well.

How It Works

1. Make the animal chart with the pockets as shown in the diagram. This chart is good for a twelve-week span. Reuse it at the end of the twelve weeks.

2. Each week has a pocket for every animal.

3. There are ten words in each pocket on a single card. You will need up to twenty cards in the pockets to accommodate the number of students who may be in that pocket at one time.

4. The easiest words are in the Chinchilla pocket 1. The hardest words are in the Elephant pocket 12. You will have to vary the difficulty of the words for each animal level and each pocket number. This is not hard because it has already been done in most spelling texts.

5. *Instructions*: If a student gets 100 percent in the spelling test two weeks in a row in one animal level of words, that student then moves down the next week to the next animal level. For example, if you get 100 percent in Aardvarks week 3 and 100 percent in Aardvarks week 4, you then move to the words in Tigers for week 5.

Week Number	1	2	3	4	5	6	7	8	9	10	11	12
Chinchillas	1 ⊐	2 ⊐	3 ⊐	4 ⊐	5 ⊐	6 ⊐	7 ⊐	8 ⊐	9 ⊐	10 ⊐	11 ⊐	12 ⊐
Aardvarks	1 ⊐	2 ⊐	3 ⊐	4 ⊐	5 ⊐	6 ⊐	7 ⊐	8 ⊐	9 ⊐	10 ⊐	11 ⊐	12 ⊐
Tigers	1 ⊐	2 ⊐	3 ⊐	4 ⊐	5 ⊐	6 ⊐	7 ⊐	8 ⊐	9 ⊐	10 ⊐	11 ⊐	12 ⊐
Wallabies	1 ⊐	2 ⊐	3 ⊐	4 ⊐	5 ⊐	6 ⊐	7 ⊐	8 ⊐	9 ⊐	10 ⊐	11 ⊐	12 ⊐
Panda Bears	1 ⊐	2 ⊐	3 ⊐	4 ⊐	5 ⊐	6 ⊐	7 ⊐	8 ⊐	9 ⊐	10 ⊐	11 ⊐	12 ⊐
Giraffes	1 ⊐	2 ⊐	3 ⊐	4 ⊐	5 ⊐	6 ⊐	7 ⊐	8 ⊐	9 ⊐	10 ⊐	11 ⊐	12 ⊐
Elephants	1 ⊐	2 ⊐	3 ⊐	4 ⊐	5 ⊐	6 ⊐	7 ⊐	8 ⊐	9 ⊐	10 ⊐	11 ⊐	12 ⊐

The beauty of this idea is that it is self-contained. Everyone is in the same program, yet it allows for individual differences.

THE HIGH FIVE CLASSROOM CONTROLLER

For a quick and effective way to settle a group of younger children, so they can quickly get on task, train the students to respond to a high five hand sign when you say to them, "Give me five." The response you want is a combination of five distinct behaviors. This is accomplished in the training process by telling the students that whenever you give and say the "high five" signal, it means:

1. All eyes are watching.

2. All ears are listening.

3. All mouths are silent.

4. All hands are still.

5. All feet are still.

Initially, it will take a while, especially for the younger ones, to respond quickly and properly. It is therefore a good idea at first to have them repeat to you the list of five behaviors as they do them.

Once they learn this simple process, it will be second nature to the students to respond correctly to the high five signal. When taught at the early grades, this idea will have staying power for other teachers as the students progress through the grades. It has been taught at the grade 1 level and was still being used effectively when those same students reached grade 6. The idea works well and everyone benefits.

THE MINI DEBATE

Teachers love to have students working and learning to the limit of their potential. Of the many programs, ideas, and concepts that will accomplish this, the Mini Debate works very well.

The Mini Debate works because it does not have a long-drawn-out, formalized debate format that takes days and even weeks to prepare. The Mini Debate is a scaled-down version of the formal procedure; it allows for more students to get involved in and enjoy the process. Units of work have time constraints. It is too difficult in the time space of a normal unit of work to have all the students in the class present formalized debates on the topic of study, given the length of the average school period.

Here is how the Mini Debate will work for you:

1. Like a formal debate, the scaled-down version is a series of verbal statements or arguments stating the pros and cons of a proposition. Propositions should be stated clearly and in the affirmative. "Be it resolved that all students should wear uniforms to school" is a good example.

2. There must be one group supporting the proposition and one group trying to defeat the proposition.

3. With the Mini Debate in the classroom, it is best to have a maximum of two students on either side. One student presents the argument for his or her side, and the other student prepares and presents the rebuttal. Positive and negative speakers normally alternate.

4. Because of the time constraints of the average class period, the presentations must have a time limit. Usually, five minutes is allowed for each side to give the pro and con of the proposition, and another five minutes for the rebuttal from each side. This uses twenty minutes of class time per set of four students.

5. Your main goal, as a teacher, in developing the Mini Debate idea is threefold:

   a. To have information presented that reinforces previous learning in a subject area.

   b. To introduce and develop the basic concepts of the debating procedure. It is purely at your discretion whether you declare one team a winner over the other.

   c. To have students learn critical thinking skills—to change their paradigm so they can see the totality of a situation, instead of focusing on just one aspect.

Advantages of the Mini Debate

1. More students can participate.

2. Preparation time for students is much less than that needed for a formal debate.

3. If you base your propositions on the material you are working on in your history, science, civics, psychology, or other classes, this will reinforce the learning of the material as the debate is presented.

4. The Mini Debate introduces all students to the basics of the formal debate. The formal debate process can then be explained to the class as a whole when interest is high.

THE TEN MOST IMPORTANT TEST-WRITING SKILLS

Students must write tests; this is a fact of academic life. There are other methods of evaluation, but by far the most common is the written test or exam. The exam is one of the best ways to find out whether a student has absorbed the necessary information.

Many students, while possessing an excellent capacity for learning knowledge, have trouble attaining high marks because they do not know how to approach the writing of a test. They do not possess the skills to work this often stressful situation to their advantage. By presenting the following concepts, you can help your students be most successful in transferring information from their intellects to the papers before them.

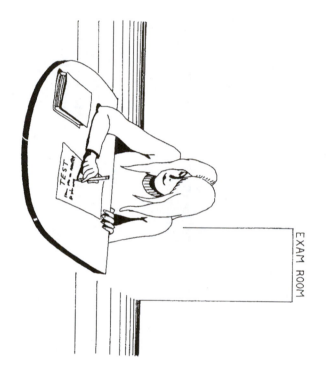

EXAM ROOM

TEST-WRITING SKILLS (COPY FOR STUDENTS)

1. Read the instructions before you start to write the test. If you do not understand or cannot read any of the directions, ask the supervisor for clarification.

2. Read the test over thoroughly before you begin writing it.

3. Put a check mark beside the questions you easily know how to do. Go back to the beginning and do those with the check marks first. This will reduce your stress level at the beginning of a test or exam.

4. Make sure your name, student number, and name of the class are clearly filled out before writing the test.

5. Manage your test time properly. The greater the mark value of a question, the greater the amount of time that should be spent on that question. Set your watch on the desk and proportion the amount of time to the number of marks per question. For example, a question worth 10 marks out of 100 should get 10 percent of the time.

6. Get a good night's sleep before writing the exam. Your intellect will not be in high gear if you stay up all night studying. Be properly prepared; study sufficiently in advance.

7. Shield your paper from others. The person correcting the test will be suspicious if there are two identical wrong answers on the papers of people who sat close to each other.

8. Bring extra pens, pencils, and other necessary materials. If calculators are permitted or are necessary, bring two—one as a backup.

9. Check your answers.

10. Hand in your test at the end of the time allowed. You may get a new idea or two that you can quickly add in at the end of the test period.

Good test-writing skills can help even the mediocre or poor student achieve a degree of success he or she has not attained before. Like many things in life, a thorough understanding of how to approach, work through, and complete a task, problem, or challenge will be of immeasurable value.

76

ROLE-PLAYING

Some teaching techniques or ideas dovetail right into students' desires or ways of thinking; role-playing is one of these. Students can be real hams when it comes to acting out a particular situation. The kitchen debate between Nixon and Khrushchev, for example, can be acted out by use of role play. Role-playing reinforces the learning of information.

Because role-playing involves two or more people physically acting out a situation or scene, the students gain a much richer understanding and memory of the situation.

Role-playing is best utilized after intense study in a subject area; this makes it great for history classes. As well, social-emotional questions can be role-played to give the students a better look at more abstract concepts, such as compassion and empathy.

There are two ways to get started. One is to have students draw a concept, historical situation, or event from a hat, and then do the role play "cold," or with no preparation. The other and more comprehensive way to do role-playing is to give the students the roles ahead of time, so they can conduct some research to do a more "polished" job.

THOUGHTS ON THE USE OF ROLE-PLAYING IN THE CLASSROOM

1. It will greatly reinforce learning, because students will more easily remember the actions and interactions of the players.

2. Students can correct (on paper) the detail errors of the participants as they are playing the roles. This information can then be used for classroom discussion.

3. It is best to make sure one or two people do not dominate the role-playing (by volunteering), but rather have students do this on a rotational basis so all get a chance to perform.

4. Role-playing develops ad-lib public speaking skills that are very important today.

5. Role-playing works best when participants are working with a real-life situation they can relate to.

6. With role-playing, you can inject "what if" statements to change the circumstance of a historical event to see what the new outcomes would be.

7. Once a problem has been role-played, the other students can discuss what transpired and offer improvements or suggestions, or even complete alternative approaches to how the problem could be resolved.

8. The role-players themselves will greatly benefit from playing the parts because they will get a feeling for the point of view of the person being played.

9. Role-playing is one of the best attention-getters of all time. While students are focusing on it, management problems are minimized.

Section Three

POSITIVE FEELINGS AND CREATIVE IDEAS

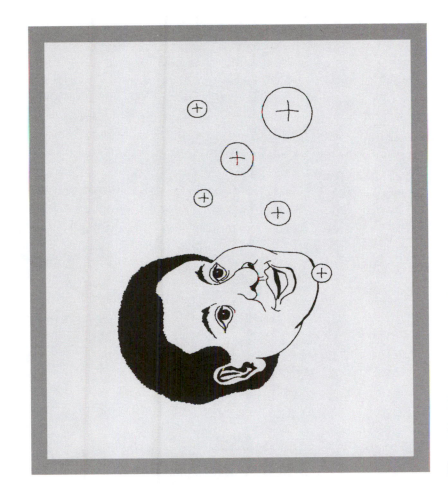

Positive reinforcement is very necessary in schools today. Some students are not in academically supportive environments when they are not in school. Many receive little, if any, encouragement from anyone, anywhere, at any time, about anything.

Gone are the days of corporal punishment and heavy-handed coercion. Indeed, it is doubtful whether these old ideas created anything other than fear, resentment and avoidance tactics in students. In today's culture, most students will respond favorably to the self-esteem enhancing concepts we present here.

Not only do we show reward and reinforcement concepts, we also offer some really neat fun ideas. The "Pot O' Gold Dirt Dessert, Environmentally Friendly Idea" is a terrific example of this—Just read it and you will see.

77 THE PENNY CARNIVAL AND FIFTY GREAT IDEAS TO HELP MAKE IT A SUCCESS

A penny carnival is one of the best money makers for the student council of your school. This event usually takes place within the school (gymnasium) and its surroundings. This carnival can also be a learning experience for many students.

The overriding consideration, of course, is safety. Teachers must look at each event and consider what the worst case scenario would be for each penny carnival idea. You must remember that Murphy's Law applies doubly to any event *you* are responsible for. If something should happen, there is a 100% chance the teacher will get some or all of the blame.

The following seven general rules of thumb of what kinds of events not to have should be followed:

1. Anything with a sharp point (e.g., darts).

2. Anything that involves heat or heat transfer.

3. Any item to be thrown at a person's face, even shaving cream.

4. A hitting event of any sort (e.g., pillow fights).

5. Eating contests of any sort.

6. Any event that puts slippery grease or soap on the floor.

7. Any event that includes shooting a projectile from a gun or a bow.

Now that we have the negatives out of the way, what can you do to have a successful penny carnival? The following guidelines will help with this:

1. When classrooms or groups start thinking of events, they should have at least one alternate idea in case their idea has already been taken.

2. Have every classroom or group sign in their event at the school office a week or two before the carnival to avoid duplication and to consider the safety of each item.

3. Assign each class or group a space in the gymnasium or other location.

4. Each class must provide their own cash box.

5. Allow only one class period immediately before the carnival for set up. Usually not more than four people are needed to set up any event.

6. The group or class must have a schedule of workers for the event or booth. This must be well monitored and rigidly adhered to. These students are to be instructed that the cash box and the event's prizes are to be secured at all times.

7. Each group should put up posters to advertise its event. These should explain event rules and prices. These posters should not be taped onto painted surfaces and should be removed immediately after the penny carnival.

8. If your event has distinct rules (e.g., stand behind a target line to throw a beanbag), these must be clearly established in advance, so there are no arguments.

155

9. Have a centrally or conveniently located adult or teacher to make change.

10. It is a good idea to invite the students from the next lower grade to the carnival if that next grade is at a different school and would normally be a feeder school to yours. This introduces those students to your facilities in a positive way and increases your cash flow.

11. It is not good to have the carnival at the junior high or high school level (300 students or under) last more than two hours. Students will run out of money and interest in that time.

12. If the penny carnival is held in the gymnasium, do not allow students to wander through the rest of the school during the proceedings.

13. Each classroom or group must have a cleanup committee.

14. All monies must be turned into the school office immediately after the carnival.

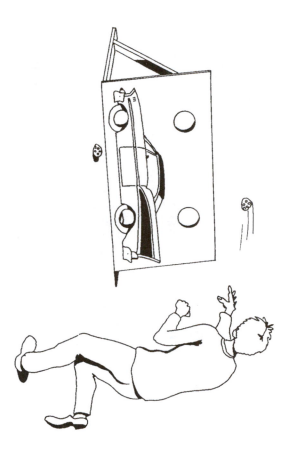

To help make your penny carnival a success, here are fifty dandy ideas for events:

1. Beanbag toss through holes pre-cut in a board.
2. Football kick through uprights (outside).
3. Saying the alphabet backwards in 30 or 60 seconds.
4. Rolling an egg to a target with your nose.
5. Water balloon toss back and forth.
6. Bounce a golf ball into a target.
7. Old walnut shell and pea game.
8. Arm wrestling contests.
9. Basketball toss to basket.

156

10. Bake sale.

11. Floating cup or pan on water. Students toss coins to land in for a prize.

12. Ring toss over stationary bottles.

13. Car racing by blowing behind a toy car.

14. Wheelbarrow races.

15. Duck pond—pick a duck; win a prize.

16. Dunk tank with adult (local celebrity) as person being dunked.

17. Three-legged races with legs tied together.

18. Walking on stilts.

19. Potato sack races—entrants pay to participate.

20. Students try to peel tape off a bottle while wearing oven mitts—30 seconds.

21. Fish pond.

22. Ants in a portable ant hill—guess the number.

23. Jelly bean guess.

24. Sell privilege to wear a hat in school during the penny carnival.

25. Batting cage—charge to hit baseballs from pitching machine.

26. Pitcher's cage—clocks speed of pitches.

27. Put nails on a board spaced about one inch apart. Drop ball bearing or washer down nail board to different cups at the bottom—different cups equal different prizes.

28. Guess the amount of chocolate chips in a cookie the size of a pie—winner gets the cookie.

29. Bash a junk car with a sledge hammer—very big money maker but must get a car donated and provide face and body protection for the students—careful supervision is mandatory.

30. Haunted house.

31. Basketball dribbling contest.

32. Hockey puck shoot to target on the floor (plastic or foam puck).

33. Tiddly winks tournament or use as a challenge in itself.

34. Football throw through hula hoop.

35. Waving a fan to move a paper fish on the floor to a circle target.

36. Balloon shaving contest. Two or three students at a time use razors to remove shaving cream from balloons. First to finish without breaking wins.

37. Bowling using plastic bowling ball and plastic pins.

38. Face painting. At the end of the carnival, line up all who had their faces painted. Have the rest of the students applaud the most for the best. The person with the most applause wins a prize.

39. Throwing baseballs through hole in apple basket or box.

40. Yard stick or meter stick balancing contest between two to ten students at a time. Each tries to balance on the top of one finger—largest time wins.

41. Rent time on computer game system.

42. Enter-to-win draws—sell tickets on donated items.

43. The great ducky neck-ring game. Have several rubber duckies floating in a basin. Students must throw sealer rings around their neck.

44. Bobbing for apples.

45. The exciting candy scramble, usually done on floor mats. Sell chances to scramble for wrapped candy. Usually four people at a time. All stand beside the person who has two handfuls of candy. When the candy is tossed onto the gym mat, all four students scramble to get as much as they can.

46. Sell grab bags.

47. Bubble gum blowing contest—usually four contestants at a time. Person to blow largest and fastest is the winner.

48. Make a spin-for-prizes board where an arrow is spun on a circular board. The arrow stops at a prize.

49. Board games contests.

50. Golf ball putt to a cup or hole in a board.

158

78

TOTALLY NEAT PUN TICKETS

You have a group of vibrant elementary students that you know will perform well with positive reinforcement. You would like these students to keep up and improve the good work pace. You, therefore, need a no cost, effective reward system to integrate into your daily classroom routine.

The reward system that you need is the Pun Ticket System. The pun tickets shown (Figure 3-1) give the student a "warm fuzzy" that is at once rewarding and amusing.

When a student has performed well or has completed some special task, you give the student a Pun Ticket as a reward. Students up to junior high school relate to pun tickets because the cute play on words is a concrete reminder that you care.

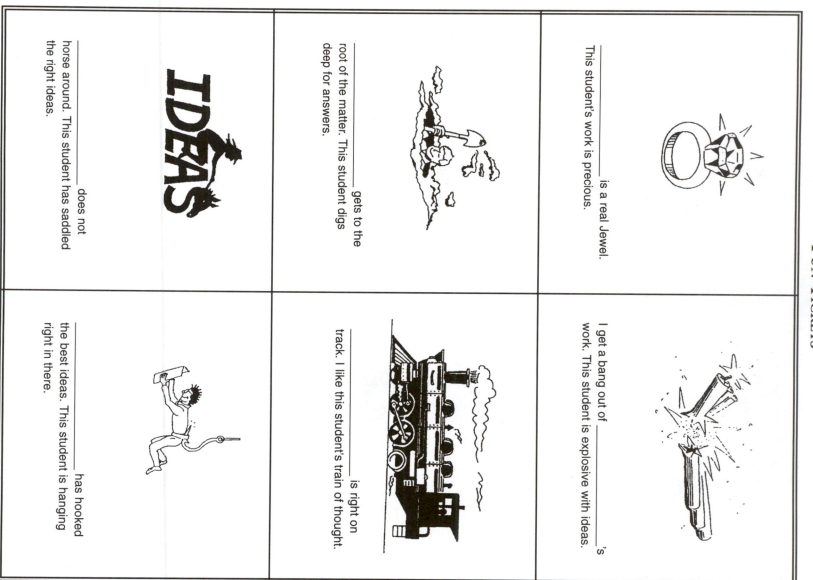

Figure 3-1
PUN TICKETS

This student's work is precious. _____ is a real jewel.

_____ gets to the root of the matter. This student digs deep for answers.

IDEAS

_____ does not horse around. This student has saddled the right ideas.

I get a bang out of _____'s work. This student is explosive with ideas.

_____ is right on track. I like this student's train of thought.

_____ has hooked the best ideas. This student is hanging right in there.

Figure 3-1 *(continued)*

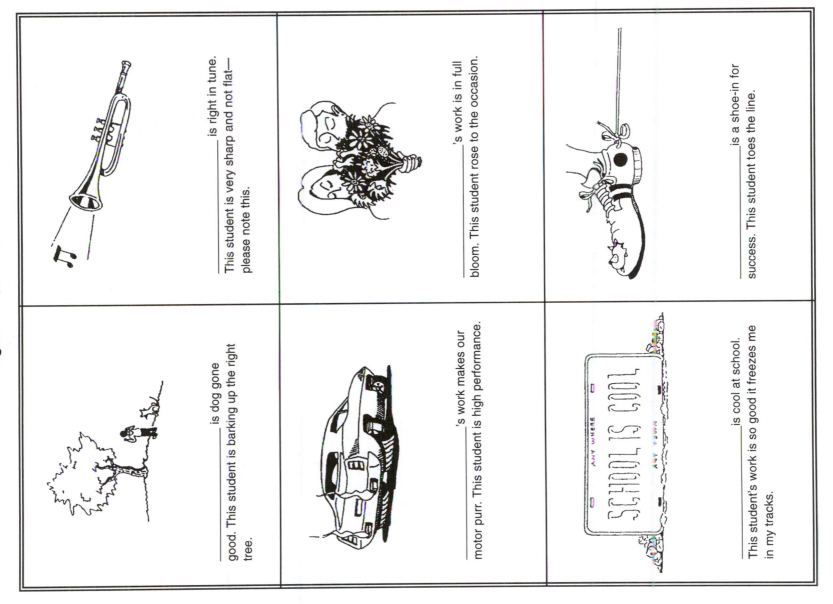

_____ is right in tune. This student is very sharp and not flat— please note this.

_____ 's work is in full bloom. This student rose to the occasion.

_____ is a shoe-in for success. This student toes the line.

_____ is dog gone good. This student is barking up the right tree.

_____ 's work makes our motor purr. This student is high performance.

_____ is cool at school. This student's work is so good it freezes me in my tracks.

SCHOOL IS COOL
ANY WHERE
ANY TOWN

79

FREE-FROM-HOMEWORK CARDS

Reward systems in their own way help you maintain discipline if the students want, or can be made to want, the reinforcement that you have. So it follows then that every teacher could use a positive reward system that works well, costs nothing and is easily implemented and understood by all.

Free-from-Homework Cards (Figure 3-2) fit the bill perfectly here. Simple in their function and zero in cost, one of these cards is exactly as the title says, it allows a student to not have to finish a particular homework assignment on a certain day or to not have to do the homework assignment whatsoever. This is at your discretion.

Like all reinforcement systems, it is not to be used without some discretion. The cards are to be used occasionally to serve you, the teacher, as a reward for good behavior, extra work performed or for special needs. The cards, of course, will become of greater value the more homework you assign and the greater the sanctions you have in place for students who are tardy in this area.

FREEDOM AT 15
IT WAS IN THE CARDS

162

Figure 3-2

FREE FROM HOMEWORK CARD

GOOD FOR: missing, skipping, not doing, failure to complete, refusing, falling short of, missing the mark on, neglecting, disregarding, losing, mislaying, misplacing, escaping from, deserting, departing from, not having a clue about, destroying, obliterating, absentmindedly forgetting, suppressing the thought of, repressing, or burying your homework one time.

☐ Student must still do the homework assignment but a delay of _____ days is given.

☐ Student does not have to do the assignment.

_____   Teacher/Supervisor

Student Name

FREE FROM HOMEWORK CARD

GOOD FOR: missing, skipping, not doing, failure to complete, refusing, falling short of, missing the mark on, neglecting, disregarding, losing, mislaying, misplacing, escaping from, deserting, departing from, not having a clue about, destroying, obliterating, absentmindedly forgetting, suppressing the thought of, repressing, or burying your homework one time.

☐ Student must still do the homework assignment but a delay of _____ days is given.

☐ Student does not have to do the assignment.

_____   Teacher/Supervisor

Student Name

80

THE ROUND 2-U

Many students are late handing in assignments. For various valid and not-so-valid reasons, students will be tardy when it comes to the due date for a particular assignment. In most cases it is not really important for you to have all the assignments in on a particular day because you likely would not have time to read all those ten-page essays in one day anyway.

How can you turn the situation around to your advantage? How can you make the handing in of an assignment late a reward tool you can use? Use the unique concept of the Round 2-U (Figure 3-3). It allows a student a specified number of days of grace when it comes to handing in a report, essay or homework assignment.

With the Round 2-U, the student will get his or her assignment "around to you" at some specified time other than the due date.

Round 2-U's must be earned. They are not to be given out freely, otherwise there would be no reason to have a due date for the assignment in the first place. The methods of earning Round 2-U's are purely at the discretion of the teacher. You may want to use them as rewards for positive behavior or for work well done. The beauty of Round 2 U's is that they cost you nothing, are highly sought after, and therefore good reinforcers for behavior or performance.

Figure 3-3
ROUND 2-U

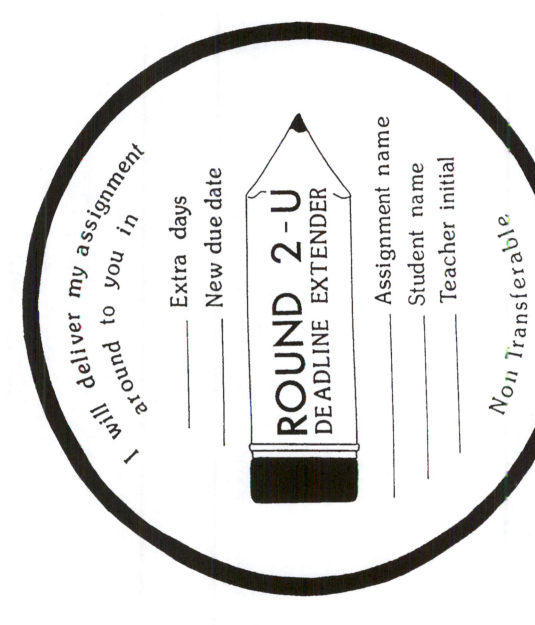

I will deliver my assignment around to you in

Extra days _____
New due date _____

ROUND 2-U
DEADLINE EXTENDER

Assignment name _____
Student name _____
Teacher initial _____

Non Transferable

81

BEHAVIOR BUCKS

You need a concrete, hands-on behavior control system that students relate to and therefore will be meaningful and effective the minute it is implemented.

What program is simple and will help keep students positive-goal oriented? The answer is Behavior Bucks (Figure 3-4). Give each student one Behavior Buck at the start of each week. Tell the students the goal of the program is for them to keep their bucks. This may not be easy for them however. The Behavior Buck will be returned to the teacher for disobeying one of the class or school rules. The rules or list of behaviors that would cause the buck to be spent should be listed on the blackboard or on a suitable bulletin board.

At the end of a time period, such as a month or term, you must provide some kind of reward system for students who keep their Behavior Bucks, such as a free period, video dance, etc. The students who have spent or squandered their Behavior Bucks by the end of the time period would normally have to get caught up on work during that time when the rewards are offered.

You may wish to have differing levels of rewards that are relative to how many Behavior Bucks a student has, or you may wish to sell privileges (e.g., wearing a hat in school) at the end of the time frame. Another good idea is to place all the remaining bucks into a draw drum for a prize or privilege.

166

Figure 3-4

BEHAVIOR BUCKS

82

THE TWENTY-FIVE-SPACE CARD SYSTEM

In the working of your classroom, you may feel the need for a positive reinforcement system that will keep students performing well and give a pleasant ambience to the classroom environment.

An idea that does this and helps maintain discipline in the classroom at the same time is the twenty-five-space card system. In order to get started with this concept, you must make photocopies of the 25-Space Card Form (Figure 3-5). Each time a student does well, he or she gets a check mark or initial from you in one of the spaces on his or her card. When a student's card is filled, he or she can purchase free time or some other reward (e.g., extra computer access) that you provide.

Whether you let the students self-check their cards when they have completed a task is at your discretion. This has been accomplished quite successfully, however, the flaws in this approach are obvious and would depend entirely on the personalities you have in your classroom.

The twenty-five-space card system works well, especially if you need a response from home. For example, if you have a test or note that needs to go home, be signed and returned, you can make the return of the signed test worth three initials or check marks. This almost assures you of getting a 100% return of the necessary information or papers.

Figure 3-5

THE 25-SPACE CARD FORM

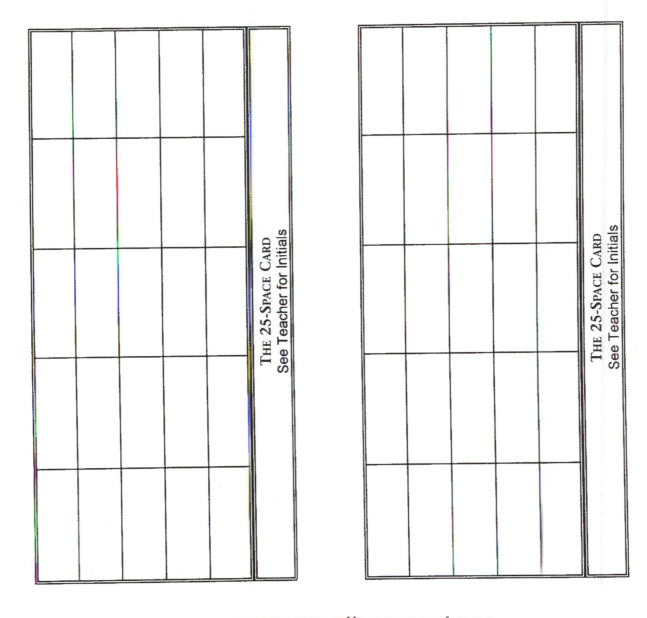

THE 25-SPACE CARD
See Teacher for Initials

THE 25-SPACE CARD
See Teacher for Initials

83

THE DOUBLE DIAMOND AWARDS

Many times when teachers would like to manage or control a classroom, they revert to punishment instead of developing a program of positive reinforcement using meaningful rewards. Positive reinforcement is of greater value to the teacher because behaviors that result from positive reinforcement are intensely more predictable than are behaviors that result from punishment.

An excellent positive reinforcement system that will pay behavior and P.R. dividends is the Double Diamond Award. With this reward system, you identify those students that meet your selected criteria (good grades, respectful behavior, improved performance, etc.), and you send each student to the office to be congratulated by the principal and be given the Double Diamond Certificate (Figure 3-6) or letter of excellence. (This is the first Diamond.)

After the presentation of the award, the principal calls the student's parents and informs them of the excellent behavior or performance of the student. (This is the second Diamond.) The beauty of the Double Diamond Award system is that it goes beyond the teacher in the classroom to the upper level of school administration, where the student sees recognition by this meaningful group. The recognition is then extended to the student's family—offering further rewards in terms of self-esteem for the student—and the P.R. value to the school is immeasurable.

Figure 3-6

Double Diamond Award

This is to certify that

_____

has won the

DOUBLE DIAMOND
AWARD

for excellent behavior and school performance

_____ principal

_____ date

84

THE ENVIRONMENTAL AWARD—
SOLVING LARGER PROBLEMS

Every school should have an environmental award. In this society, there is an ever-increasing consciousness of the fragility of the environment we all share. It is important, therefore, to create an awareness in our students of the need to preserve and respect the natural surroundings.

To this end, the environmental award has its place or value. This award would normally be given out on the school awards night at the end of each semester or year to the student who has displayed the greatest respect and understanding of environmental issues. That respect and understanding would have manifested itself not only in school written work but in community or school related action in this area.

ENVIRONMENTAL AWARD GUIDELINES

1. Information about the award should be presented to the students at an assembly near the start of each year or semester.

2. Students should be told to target this award in terms of essay topics, report themes, and oral presentations.

3. Due to the increasing awareness of the importance of environmental issues, it may be possible to have a local service club or organization enrich the award with a cash donation.

4. The award should be applied for because the application form can show the student's environmental awareness outside of the school confines, as well as describe the actions of the student inside the school itself. The application can show the depth of the student's commitment to this area, and will also ensure that those who sincerely desire and deserve this accolade are the ones to get it. There will be less chance of a frivolous response to its receipt if the student had put effort into an application.

A quick study of the Environmental Award Application Form (Figure 3-7) reveals a focus on four basic areas:

a. A look at the student's philosophical base by asking the "why" question.

b. The extent of the student's involvement in school and community activities.

c. A description of leadership roles the student has assumed in the area of environmental issues.

d. A description of the academic work or projects the student has completed or taken part in.

172

Figure 3-7
The Environmental Award
Application Form

Name: _____   Date: _____

Please be as detailed as possible. Use extra paper if necessary.

1. Explain why you are interested in environmental issues.

_____

_____

_____

_____

2. Describe how you have participated in school and community environmental issues. Stress any leadership roles you have assumed in this area.

_____

_____

_____

3. Outline any research, report, essays or other school work you have completed that reflects your environmental interests.

_____

_____

_____

_____

85

POSI-NOTES—A GOOD THING; CHEAP TOO!

There are days when everyone in school needs a lift. These are the routine work stretches during which everyone including the class goldfish has an advanced case of the doldrums. It is at times like these that you need a positive reinforcer that will raise everyone's spirits instantly. It is also essential that this reinforcer is easy to implement and costs you nothing.

You need Posi-Notes. In order to get the ball rolling on this idea, each student must be given photo copies of the Posi-Note Form (Figure 3-8). It is necessary for each individual to have one copy for each other student in the class. If there are twenty-eight students in the class, each person will fill out twenty-seven Posi-Note forms.

On the posi-notes, the students are to write something nice or positive about each other member of the class. Once all the forms have been completed by all the students, they are to be distributed to each individual by one or two mail persons. What, in effect, occurs is that each student in a class of twenty-eight would receive twenty-seven positive or happy thoughts from others in the classroom.

Included here are two different posi-note styles. They both have lead sentences to give the students a point of view or direction from which to work.

The first style requires students to tell the other person something nice about what that person does. The other style requires the students to say something positive or uplifting about what the other person is. The style you use will depend on the nature of the class you are teaching. It may be advantageous to give the students a choice.

174

Figure 3-8

POSITIVE NOTE FORMS

POSITIVE NOTE

To: _____

From: _____

This is what I like about what you do:

_____

_____

_____

_____

_____

_____

POSITIVE NOTE

To: _____

From: _____

This is what I like about who you are:

_____

_____

_____

_____

_____

_____

THE PRO-MERIT SYSTEM

Teachers, administrators, and students enjoy a good positive reward system that works to control errant behavior yet, at the same time, is not weighted down with heavy negative connotations like fear of loss of privileges or of corporal punishment.

An ideal example of a school-based positive reward program is the Pro-Merit System, whereby students gain merit points for behavior or performance.

With this system, students are told at the start of the year or term that if they do well in a listed set of areas of school life in a given month or designated time period, they would be given merit points. Students would have to obtain a certain number of those merit points in order to participate in a monthly pro-merit gathering. That gathering of students could be anything from a school dance—perhaps a Sock Hop—to an ice cream party put on by the parents. This gathering would usually take place in the last period of the month. Students would need to meet a certain level (at your discretion) of attained merit points each month in order to attend the gathering.

The objective of the pro-merit system is two-fold. First, it is to be used to control or target behaviors that need to be corrected or strengthened, and it is designed to show students that ultimately, students are responsible for their own actions.

Behaviors, such as being late for school, of course, would not gain a student any merit points, but he or she would not lose any either. Unlike the de-merit system, the Pro-Merit System does not allow for the taking away of merit points. This is not unlike the world of work in some instances; if a worker is not at work on a given day, he or she does not get paid. No wages are taken off from previous work completed, but nothing is added to the paycheck, whereas the workers who were on the job would benefit from the merit of their regular pay. You are paying students for good behavior with merit points.

Use the following list of behavior areas for which merit points can be earned. There may be some differences to suit your particular school, but generally speaking, these are the areas that are most universal and could most easily be used as targeted behaviors:

1. Regular attendance—no unexplained absences.
2. No lates—school or class.
3. Assignments completed and handed in on time.
4. Record of good responsible behavior.

The only real problem with this system is in the tallying of points. To avoid adding to your workload by recording every good thing, it is much easier to tally all the lates, poor behavior, etc., in your targeted areas because they are recorded already and are much less likely to occur than the good things. A simple total of these negatives on a student's record will show you where to not add merit points to a student's record. This could be done once a week to show students a running total.

Two elements must be in place for the pro-merit system to function properly. The first is that the reward of the promerit gathering must be viable and meaningful to the students. The second is that a certain amount of advertising must be in place in order to

176

© 1998 by The Center for Applied Research in Education

promote the program. The greater the visibility, the greater will be the response to it. To facilitate this, the pro-merit gathering can be advertised with posters and other appropriate media—for example: "Video Games Day, November 15."

It helps to record the tally of merit points on a highly visible chart that is updated each week. The preparation legwork for the rewards can be accomplished by the students, thus minimizing your workload.

Students not attending the pro-merit gathering because they did not have enough points must remain in the classroom or other supervised area to get caught up on work not completed because of their behavior.

177

EARNED FIVE-MINUTE FREE-TIME CARDS

Teachers need quick, efficient, low-cost reward systems that will serve to motivate, stimulate and give "warm fuzzies" to the students as they progress through the school day. Teachers have the control over time and what students do or perform in that segment of time, and they can develop reward systems. The Earned Five-Minute Free-Time Card (Figure 3-9) is a classic example.

These cards allow individuals or groups of students to have five minutes of unstructured time at specified periods during the day.

GUIDELINES TO HELP YOU IMPLEMENT FIVE-MINUTE FREE-TIME CARDS

1. The cards must be earned by whatever criteria you establish. You may want to give them out for excellent achievement in a subject area or for performing some special task.

2. It is important that the student exercising his or her Five-Minute Free-Time Card be supervised at all times. If a student is allowed to go to the school library or to work at a computer or play station while others are doing a regular assignment, that student must be under the watchful eye of a teacher or responsible supervisor.

3. It is at your discretion whether or not you want to let the Five-Minute Free-Time Cards build up to ten, fifteen or even more minutes of free time. Some students can handle this, but others cannot.

It is important, in terms of discipline and classroom control, that the Five-Minute Free-Time Cards be used to solve the problem of providing a meaningful, low-cost reward system. Like all reinforcement techniques or processes, the cards should not be used liberally or without justification. Used properly, the Five-Minute Free-Time Cards can be a wonderful tool to reward and reinforce positive behavior and school performance.

178

Figure 3-9

Earned Five-Minute Free-Time Card

Five-Minute Free-Time Card

The owner of this card had earned FIVE (5) MINUTES of "**free**" school time from _____

Teacher's Name

This card must be spent wisely in a supervised location.

Five-Minute Free-Time Card

The owner of this card had earned FIVE (5) MINUTES of "**free**" school time from _____

Teacher's Name

This card must be spent wisely in a supervised location.

THE NUT-AND-BOLT REWARD SYSTEM

The idea presented here is one of the oldest reward tricks or systems in the book. Students respond to reward systems if they are administered properly and consistently. They work much better if there is some kind of meaningful, tangible reinforcement awaiting their proper performance of duties.

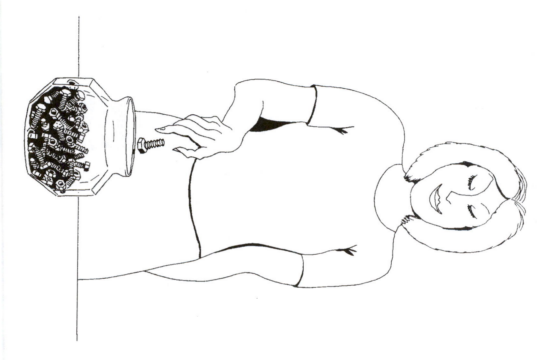

HOW THE NUT-AND-BOLT REWARD SYSTEM WORKS

1. Start with a plastic jar (the size is at your discretion) and enough nuts and bolts of the same size to fill the jar.

2. Explain to the students (usually on opening day), that you will evaluate each day in terms of the quality of learning that went on. If it was a very good day, you will

180

add a bolt to the jar. If the day was only so-so, you will add only a nut, which is much smaller than a bolt, and therefore occupies less space in the jar.

On days when behavior was poor and the learning process was not as strong as it could be, you tell the students that neither a nut or bolt will be added to the jar that day.

3. Students are then told that once the jar is full of nuts and bolts, you will provide some kind of meaningful reward, such as extra gym or computer time or perhaps even have an ice cream day. One teacher I know makes a twelve layered cake for the occasion when the jar is full.

It soon becomes apparent to the students that it is more profitable to have a very good learning day, which results in a bolt's being placed in the jar, than it is to have a mediocre day, when only a nut is put in. Worst of all—and to be avoided at all costs—is a poor learning day, when the jar does not receive any booty.

Place the jar right in front of the students on your desk or on a nearby filing cabinet. This makes the students constantly aware of their need to have a very good learning day in order to please you and maximize the number of bolts in the jar. Soon, you will find students policing themselves, especially after one or two reward days.

Some teachers use marbles instead of nuts and bolts to fill the jar. To allow for good and mediocre days, two different sizes of marbles would have to be used.

181

THE POT O' GOLD, DIRT DESSERT, ENVIRONMENTALLY FRIENDLY IDEA

When teaching day in and day out, the routine—while never getting to the point of humdrum—sometimes needs a refreshing program to stimulate and interest everyone concerned. The Pot O' Gold, Dirt Dessert, Environmentally Friendly Idea is perfect here.

This is basically a reward system that is coupled to an environmental awareness concept that will reinforce the work skills of the students plus give them a consciousness of the need to preserve, conserve, and recycle.

How THE IDEA WORKS

1. First set up a Pot O' Gold display in your classroom by spraying an old pot flat black. Then take sixty or so medium-sized rocks and spray paint these a gold color. Place the gold "nuggets" beside the pot in a conspicuous spot on a shelf.

2. Students are then allowed to place one gold nugget into the pot any time their performance or behavior is exceptional. The criteria you use to allow students to place a nugget in the pot is at your discretion, but here are a few suggestions:

   ➡ When a student does a super job on an assignment.

   ➡ When a student gets 100% on a test.

   ➡ When someone goes out of his or her way to do something for a classmate or others.

   ➡ When students play cooperatively in gym class.

   ➡ When lockers or desks are all neat and orderly for a period of time.

3. Individual work and cooperative work are all used to fill the pot.

4. When the Pot O' Gold is *nearly* filled, the class can then enjoy a "Pot O' Gold" party. However, to get to the party, the students must fill in the remaining nuggets into the pot. This is accomplished by having an "environmental awareness day" in the community, so the last few nuggets can be placed into the Pot O' Gold. With an environmental awareness day, you take the students (with parents' help) out into the community (if suitable) to do one or more of the following tasks:

   ➡ Clean a yard for a senior citizen.

   ➡ Collect old newspapers, phone books, etc., to be recycled.

   ➡ Volunteer to clean a local park or sports field.

   ➡ Clean the school yard.

5. When returning to the school, continue with the environmental theme by preparing them a cake or other pastry made out of crumbs of dark chocolate cookies (the ones with the cream in the center). This is your "dirt" dessert. There is also a cookies and cream type of ice cream available to add to the dirt dessert treat. While the students are enjoying the "dirt" dessert, etc., show an environmentally supportive video. This will keep the students focused. Finally, if you think that the environment of your body can handle the calories in the dirt dessert, indulge yourself.

SWITCH A KID

You have just started the first day with a new class of students. You want to get to know their names as quickly as possible. If you are a substitute teacher entering a class you have never covered before. You would naturally need to know the students' names in a hurry. By your experience you know that some students will give you the wrong names because they think it's a "fun" thing to do.

How can you quickly memorize student names and indeed make this situation into a game?

HOW TO "SWITCH A KID"

Just after you introduce yourself, tell the students that you are going to play the game of "Switch a Kid" with them. This, in itself, will help prevent students from giving the wrong names because names are now part of a game.

As each student gives you his or her name, you repeat the name to that student directly. Once you have gone through the whole class, you then tell the students to quietly switch desks or seats with another student, as you cover your eyes with your hands. When you cover your eyes, count out loud to five, then remove your hands. You then try to remember everyone's name by repeating each name to each student.

This game of "Switch a Kid" is a fun way, with a purpose, to start school. It will set the tone for positive interaction as well as give you good solid rapport with all the students.

If the situation allows, you can use "Switch a Kid" as a memory developer for the students. In this case, each student would give out his or her middle name. You would then ask a student, or students, to stand in front of the class and cover his or her eyes as all the rest of the students quickly switch desks or chairs. The student then would remove his or her hands and try to remember everyone's middle name. This little game would give the students some idea of the difficulty you have when it comes to memorizing their names.

183

ONE-BREAK CARDS

Some behavior modification techniques are simple, effective, and easy to implement in the classroom. One-Break Cards (figure 3-10) help facilitate the flow of the work from the student to the teacher by minimizing problems and allowing students to have a small degree of power over a situation.

The One-Break Cards are just that; they allow students to have a break or to have freedom from a consequence, such as a penalty for a minor problem or rule infraction. Things like handing in an assignment late or having a messy desk or locker would fit the one-break criteria.

FUNCTIONAL IDEAS TO HELP YOU IMPLEMENT ONE-BREAK CARDS

1. The One-Break Cards are usually classroom specific and would not be used to override any school rules.

2. These cards must be earned. They can be given for quality extra work, completion of meaningful tasks or as a reward for helping others. The reasons or list of tasks you have the students earn the cards for is purely a discretionary call on your part.

3. A list of appropriate minor errant behaviors that One-Break Cards could be used for must be placed on a wall or bulletin board. If you do not list the behaviors applicable, then you run the risk of students trying to manipulate you, so they can use the cards for more serious offenses that need to be dealt with in some other way. It must always remain the teacher's prerogative to override this list should circumstances make it necessary.

4. A One-Break Card many times will act as a safety valve for the students. It allows them to buy a little time or to avoid a minor consequence; it shows that you care and are willing to be fair.

5. Be sure students do not come to rely on One-Break Cards in order to avoid work or to flout authority.

6. One-Break Cards should be used within one school year or semester. They can be carried over from one term to the next, but it is not practical to allow students to use them beyond that time frame.

Figure 3-10

ONE-BREAK CARD

This card allows you to avoid the consequences of one classroom problem as listed.

No negotiation will take place. It is 100% up to the teacher whether or not you can use this card for the purpose you specify.

_____ _____
Student's Name   Date

_____
Purpose

Teacher will place initials on

_____ YES or _____ NO

92

POSITIVE SPEAK

Many students never hear a word of encouragement, never hear a positive statement about themselves—or even get a simple "thank you" from anyone in their sphere of influence. In actual fact, many students are spoken to in a negative manner a great deal of the time. The problem here is that speaking negatively has its own momentum. If a student is verbally made to feel bad because of his or her poor behavior, that bad feeling leads to more poor behavior which leads to more reprimands. The classic vicious circle is created.

To counteract this vicious circle, every teacher must develop the skill of speaking positively. You must creat for yourself a "lifestyle of words"—learn to talk in an affirmative manner during your daily interactions with the students. This is especially important when you are conversing with the most intense behavior-problem student in the school.

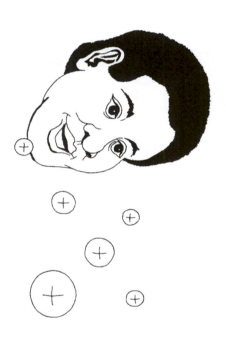

The whole concept of speaking positively can be summed up in the words of the first-century writer, St. Paul: "Do not use harmful words in talking. Use only helpful words, the kind that build up and provide what is needed, so that what you say will do good to those who hear you."

A habit of positive, upbeat language can be developed. You will find that once you can "key" your positive statements to the nature of your classroom, you will be developing a rapport with the students that will gain dividends for you in terms of improved behavior and better-quality responses. Positive speak must be sincere. There is nothing the students can spot quicker than a phoney. Your credibility will rise in the eyes of the students if you mean what you say.

Statements like the following, while somewhat unusual, are affirmative and conversation starters that build up the students.

- ➡ "Bill, I see you look cool today!"
- ➡ "Look at Judy there; she is what cool is."

186

⬆ "You're a good man, right, Mike?!"

⬆ "Hey, Kathy, I like your skills."

Uplifting statements like these can be said as the result of good performance, but they can also be used alone—"out of the blue." They do not need a good lead-in.

This concept of speaking positively is very important because a lot of times students will get into some kind of problem, hassle or crisis with some other person throughout their routine at school. When a verbal "dressing down" occurs, the positive words you gave to the child will come back to the student as savings and consciously the student will say to himself or herself, "I can't be all bad. Mrs. Jones still likes me." In this way you have created a basis for positive self-talk. Researchers have shown that what a student says to him or herself has a tremendous effect on the academic performance of that student.

With positive speak, you are having a wonderful impact on a student's self-esteem. Once you become noted as a broker of positive reinforcement, that positiveness will come back to you. "You reap what you sow."

Section Four

CONCEPTS THAT PROTECT AND TECHNIQUES THAT HELP

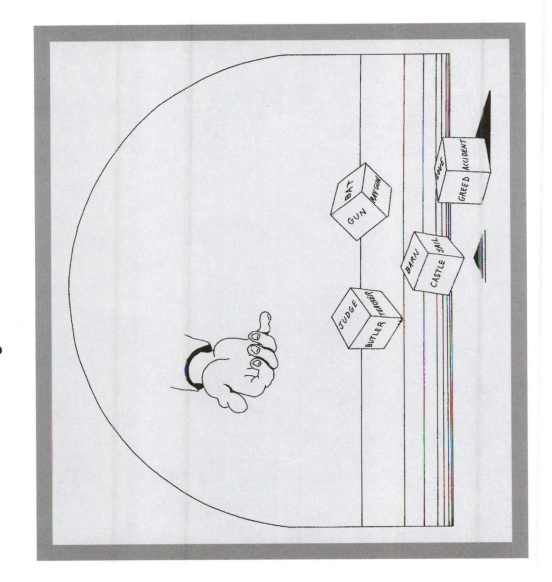

We all need to be protected in our positions as teachers if we are to function for the benefit of students. The idea called Protect Yourself—Read This, in this section, will make you aware of the intensity of problems that can occur at school. In addition, it offers you a way of protecting yourself if litigation ever comes your way. Other strategies in this section are a genuine help in the day-to-day process of teaching. The ideas in Plot Chart and Plot Dice will give a boost to any creative writing lesson by providing needed insights with which to get started. These ideas are strong and solid—"where the rubber meets the road" in education.

FIFTY STRATEGIES AND SURVIVAL GUIDELINES
FOR THE FIRST-YEAR TEACHER

Adjusting to a new profession, a new school, and a new set of responsibilities can be an uplifting experience in a teacher's life—a time of strong personal growth and positive social development.

Teaching is unlike any other profession; you have a direct and lasting influence on the lives of many people. Because of the importance of teaching, societies and cultures have a need for strong, stable, and reliable people in their classrooms. The following set of guidelines will help the first-year teacher fulfill that mandate.

1. The main concern of school jurisdictions is that a teacher have behavior control of the class. Even the most intellectually gifted and academically qualified person will be useless to the students if he or she does not have classroom management. It is best, therefore, if you adopt a policy of "fair firmness" in terms of discipline for the first few weeks of your teaching.

   Do not have "play days" or other unstructured periods during the start-up time. It is easier to lessen the firmness as school goes on than to try to gain that firmness after being relaxed. Depending on the nature of the class, it may be necessary to maintain a strong, fair but firm, policy all year long.

2. Have your lessons well prepared; know what you are talking about. While it is possible to "shoot from the hip" or "ad-lib" your lessons, it is definitely not recommended. The students will know you are unprepared and are more likely to be behavior problems as a result.

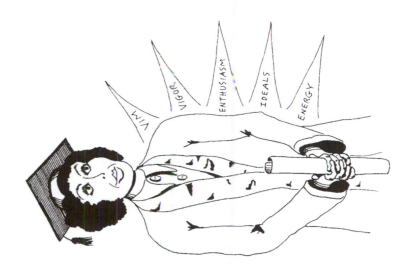

191

3. Make your "No" a "No" and your "Yes" a "Yes." If you are consistent with these two words, students will not question you when you say them. If you are wishy-washy, the students will work on you.

4. Hook up with two colleague mentors even if they are in another school jurisdiction. One should be near your own age with at least one year's experience and the other should be older and much more experienced. Consciously seek them out and ask for advice.

5. Dress comfortably but appropriately.

6. Wear proper shoes. A pair of good-quality shoes with a solid arch support will do wonders to lessen fatigue.

7. If it is possible, have a nap after school for an hour or so. Winston Churchill did this during the darkest days of the Battle of Britain. He said he "could make two days out of one by having this little snooze."

8. If your first teaching assignment is in a smaller town, work at being part of the community; you must avoid the "wallow syndrome." This occurs when several people new to an area get together and complain to each other about the community. They do not take part in any of the goings-on of that community, and by the end of the school year they have talked themselves into leaving.

It is best, therefore, to join or start a sports team (volleyball, for example), join a church or synagogue, get a hobby or take a class, join an orchestra or band—find something in the community to do.

9. Read the cumulative files or past records of your students.

10. Maintain your professional distance; be friendly, but do not become "best buds" or "pals" with your students.

11. Use the seating plan to maneuver the behavior problems and talkers away from their peers.

12. Do not work late at night alone at the school. If you do not have a choice about this, invest in a wearable cellular phone and some sort of personal alarm system.

13. Start a scrapbook of your teaching career.

14. If your school parking lot has a lot of student flow through or near it, do not park your new car with the new paint job close to where someone can "key" it.

15. Do not be intimidated by the glowing reports of the "marvelous" teacher who was in the position before you. He or she had faults and inconsistencies, too. People tend to forget the bad and remember the good. You are not filling someone else's shoes; you are making your own path.

16. Keep an absorbent cloth in your desk drawer. You have no idea how often you will use it to wipe spills, clean a spot off your suit, or solve some unique problem.

17. Keep a box of band-aids in your desk drawer. Put a band-aid in your wallet or purse.

18. Use a stapler that has a universal size of staples.

192

19. Keep a box of chalk on or in your desk.

20. Write the daily assignments on the side of the chalkboard that is not often used.

21. Wear a pen around your neck.

22. Get an influenza shot. You will be exposed to a multitude of bacteria.

23. Have a lockable drawer or filing cabinet.

24. Keep a multidrive screwdriver and a pair of pliers in your lockable drawer.

25. Secure your mark or grades lists, especially before term report cards are due. Make photocopies of the marks and take these home.

26. Keep a bale or bundle of 8-1/2" × 11" white bond paper nearby.

27. Make a list of "School Guidelines or Rules" that students can easily read, so there are no arguments on these points.

28. Allow no area of your classroom to be out of your field of vision.

29. Allow only one student of the same sex to go to the washroom at one time.

30. If you keep a first-aid kit in your class, use it only up to your level of competence.

31. Keep a pair of rubber gloves in your desk drawer. Put them on when dealing with any student body fluids, or if you must help with a sick or injured student.

32. Keep an extra set of keys for your car, house, and school in a secure area that you can easily access without those keys.

33. Keep a "Things to Do" notepad on your desk.

34. If you are unsure of the ramifications of a situation, do not verbally ask advice from the office, but rather, send a note via a runner. The note should have an area on the bottom that says "Response"; that way, you have a written record of the administration's desires regarding that situation.

35. Make a distinct seating plan for every class. If there is a serious problem, this seating plan can be used for evidence as part of the normal process of a litigation.

36. When you first start teaching, you may find that the students will be generally well behaved. This, however, might not reflect their true personalities. The behavior patterns of the first few weeks could be vastly different once the novelty has worn off. Be prepared to adjust your discipline procedures any time between two weeks to a month after school has begun.

37. When doing a hands-on project (e.g., building a kite), go through everything step by step from beginning to end. Do not explain the start of the project and have everyone do it, then explain the second stage and have everyone do it. Students perform at different rates of speed and at different skill levels.

38. Have a seating plan for everything, even when students are sitting on the rug to watch television. This allows you to control where personalities are. It is much easier to prevent a problem than to have to deal with its resolution.

39. When a student—or the parent of a student—complains about another, tell the person complaining to put it in writing and sign it.

40. Never give credence to circumstantial evidence.

41. Eat a proper breakfast. It is truly the most important meal of the day.

42. Be prepared for parent-teacher interviews; have examples of the student's work to back up your grade for that child.

43. Thoroughly learn the computer system at your school.

44. Use recipe cards and a recipe card box to keep anecdotal records on students.

45. If a student refuses to write a test, have him or her write you a note telling you why.

46. Keep a file on behavior problems or on a student with hyper-critical parents.

47. If you have only one TV/VCR for your floor or area, create a booking system that all can live with.

48. Organize your classroom in responsibility areas. Assign students to look after an area; duties can include picking up papers, cleaning chalkboards, and organizing shelves.

49. Look over the curriculum before you begin. This is important at every level. You must pace yourself and the students in order to cover the necessary data. In many cases, you can inform the students of the pace, so there are no surprises.

50. If you set your own timetable for the day, make your periods about 35 to 40 minutes long. This gives a reasonable amount of time to cover a topic or subject with a degree of quality instruction.

STICKY LABELS—RECORDS ON THE WRIST

Teachers must supervise students. Some schools require teachers to keep anecdotal records of student behaviors during those supervision times. How can this recording be achieved in an efficient manner, when it is difficult to remember the details of incidents after supervision is over?

One way to have a precise anecdotal record of events that occur on supervision is to write the data on sticky labels (like the name tags used at conferences). You can carry these labels with you or—better still—wrap them around the opposite wrist from your writing hand. Whenever an incident occurs or the behavior of a student is noted, simply jot down the relevant data on the sticky label. After supervision, remove the label from the roll and stick it either in a day book in the staff room or in the student's cumulative file. Because the labels are self-adhesive, it makes them effortless to manage, quick to put into place, and easy to refer to. When the next person is on supervision, he or she can look into the day book at the labels from the last day to see what to watch for on that day's supervision.

Over a period of time, certain students will have a build-up of "stickies" in their cumulative files or in the day book. This record is invaluable when it becomes necessary to speak to the parents, either at a special meeting or during parent-teacher conferences.

The labels can also be used to record behavior and performance in the classroom. Remove them at the end of each day and place them in your record-keeping system.

THE DEWEY DECIMAL BOOK ORGANIZER BINGO

You are the school librarian, and it is your mandate to make sure that all returned books are reshelved as quickly as possible. Each book must have its proper card placed in the pocket at the back of the book before it is reshelved.

The mountain of books before you would give Sir Edmund Hillary a run for his money. How can you quickly identify what card goes with what book and have it reshelved in the shortest period of time possible? Play Dewey Decimal Bingo. (*Note:* The game works just as well with the Library of Congress cataloging system; simply change the name.) You will need a minimum of four students who know the cataloging system. Each of the students is given an approximately equal number of books on a table. Students are to place the books spine up so the Dewey Decimal number can be easily read. If possible, the books should be placed in ascending or descending numerical order, but this is not necessary.

Once the students are standing behind their piles of books, read off the number on the first card. The students then survey the spines of the books they have in front of them and yell "Bingo" if they have the book possessing that number. The card is then given to the student to place in the book pocket.

You may want to have shelf runners to work with the students who are placing the cards in the books. Those shelf runners simply take the books and put them in the correct place on the shelf. This idea will speed up your reshelving of library books by leaps and bounds.

As an alternative to the system above, have the books in front of you and the students standing at tables with the cards spread in front of them. When you read the number on the spine of the book, the student surfs the cards for the right one and yells "Bingo" when he or she has found it. The student or a runner takes the card, places it in the book pocket, and reshelves the book.

THE FRIENDSHIP CLUB

Some students do not fit in with the others. Many times, these students can be observed wandering about or crouched in a corner beside the lockers, avoiding eye contact, when others are surrounded by talkative peers. These students can have anti-social tendencies and become a behavior problem, but more likely, they will become targets for the peer-group-backed bully, or be ignored—to their personal detriment.

These students have the right to be protected and treated as persons of worth in the school. To help such students overcome feelings of shyness or social inadequacies, and to develop some needed interpersonal skills, start a "Friendship Club." This club is, in effect, a gathering together of all the students in the school who would benefit from positive social interaction.

Once students have been targeted, you need a teacher or lay person from the community to volunteer to set up and run the Friendship Club in a room at the school. The identified students are then required to report there as soon as they arrive at school, at recess, or at special activities. This club operates with two basic functions—as a rap center for these students to talk out their problems, thus creating social interaction, or as an arts and crafts work room where the students can work on various projects.

The beauty of this Friendship Club is fourfold.

1. You have removed the loners from the potential of being picked on or looked down on by others in the hall areas.

2. You are gathering together a group of students who have similar problems and can begin to create positive peer contacts in a supervised setting.

3. You are allowing these students a place where they can vent frustrations, needs, and desires in a socially acceptable setting.

4. You are placing these students in a situation where they can get a feeling of accomplishment from what they are creating.

A note of caution is in order here. Care should be taken to ensure that these students are not seen to be singled out by the other students; this would only add to their problems. A little finesse in selection and application of this program will go a long way to help these socially nonagressive children.

197

THE SITTING TEDDY

Some ideas genuinely protect the psychic space of students. These ideas can be unique, and they often range across the educational spectrum. One idea that helps the very youngest student is the Sitting Teddy.

Some children are afraid to ask to go to the restroom. This problem is more prevalent at the start of a school year, with the kindergarten and grade 1 students. The resultant accidents are a familiar thing to many an early childhood teacher. To avoid the fear of asking in these young children, use the Sitting Teddy idea.

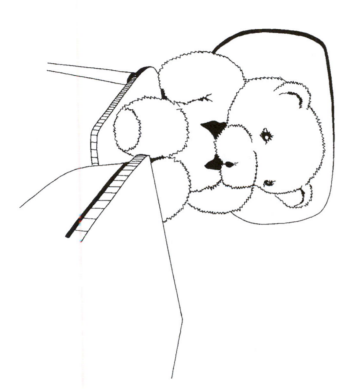

If the Sitting Teddy is to work, you need one or two regular-sized teddy bears and a chair or two in the corner for them to sit on. When a youngster needs to go to the restroom, that student simply goes to the chair and takes the teddy bear to his or her desk seat or chair and places it in a sitting position. Instruct the children that they are to feel free to get the teddy bear when they want to go to the restroom. Say, "Anytime I look at your desk, I will always know where you are because the teddy will be in your place." This is especially important for young students with bladder control problems.

An added control feature is that you decide how many teddy bears you want for this purpose; you control the number of students using the restroom at any one time.

UP-FRONT ASSIGNMENT CHART

When you are developing a unit on a topic such as "The Life of Abraham Lincoln" or on a novel study, a certain amount of student work will be assigned. You want your students to be on task and responsible for those assignments. You want your students to avoid placing responsibility for missed assignments onto you or someone else.

How can you cause students to have ownership of what they are supposed to do? To facilitate ownership and promote communication about assignments to students, photocopy the Up-Front Assignment Chart (Figure 4-1).

On this chart, students are to write the description, size or number of pages required, due date, and materials or work package number, if necessary, for the assignment associated with the unit.

This chart will normally reside at the front of a student's binder where it is less likely to get lost.

ADVANTAGES OF THE UP-FRONT ASSIGNMENT CHART

1. It is much easier to keep track of assignments. Students can quickly refer to the chart to see what must be worked on.

2. If students write in the details of assignments, there is no need for you to photocopy assignment sheets for them. You will, however, have to walk around to scan each assignment sheet—to make sure students wrote down the correct data from the chalkboard.

3. This assures all concerned that the student received notice of the assignment; students cannot say they had no knowledge of what work was due.

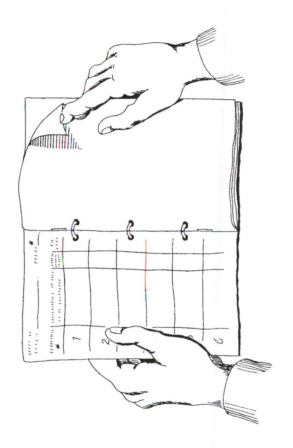

4. If parents are informed of the location of the chart in the students' binders, they can easily refer to this spot to see what assignments must be completed.

5. When the student writes his or her materials package number on the chart, that student acknowledges receiving the work packet. If an assignment is not completed, a student cannot say he or she did not receive the information.

6. Students will be able to work at an individualized pace.

7. You can individualize the charts to add enrichment or remedial programs.

8. Several assignments on the same topic or unit can be put on one chart.

200

Figure 4-1
Up-Front Assignment Chart

Student's Name: _____

Assignment Description	Size or Number of Pages	Due Date	Materials or Work Package Number

STRING ALONG WITH ME

It is often difficult to get students to stand in front of their peers to practice or reinforce impromptu public speaking skills. This great little speech-starter idea is sure to garner everyone's attention right away. This technique will help students "break the ice" when it comes to presenting themselves and their ideas before a large group of people—but there are strings attached.

How It Works

1. You need a ball of good, old-fashioned, hard-to-break string.

2. Tell the students they have a public speaking assignment and the topic is "themselves"—a subject they should have had some experience with.

3. Give the ball of string out to the first student and tell that student to cut off as much as she or he wants, but not too much. That first student then hands the string to the next student, and so on, until every person has a piece of string.

4. As soon as every student has a piece of string, tell the students that each one must get up in front of the class and talk about himself or herself while slowly wrapping the string around his or her index finger. (You will have to give a demonstration of the speed required.)

5. If the student refuses to wrap the string at the pace you demonstrated, then you wrap it around your finger as the student speaks.

6. Quite often, the most boisterous will have taken the most string, and therefore will get to speak the longest.

7. Of course, the basic rules for a speech audience must be enforced by you. These are:
   - No put-downs or Bronx cheers.
   - No coughing or excessive clearing of the throat while a person is speaking.
   - No breaking or cutting of the string before speaking.

8. Collect the string immediately after the speech, so it cannot be used as a weapon of some sort.

202

THE PLOT CHART AND PLOT DICE

100

Teachers and others spend a great deal of time trying to get students to be creative in language arts or writing skills. Teachers often encounter these kinds of responses from students when they present a creative writing assignment: "I can't think of anything to write about" or "I don't know what to say." These and similar responses come to you for various valid and not-so-valid reasons. In any event, your role is to stimulate the creative process.

Story elements of character, setting, method, and motive can be presented to students in either of two different formats. From these elements, students have the basis for writing or creating a story.

The first approach is to use the Creative Writing Plot Chart (Figure 4-2). This particular plot chart is designed to create detective or mystery stories. A student simply looks at the first element beside "person" to choose a character for his or her story. Next, the student chooses a setting the story will take place in. A method or "modus operandi" comes third, and finally the student combines these three with a motive or a reason for the action of the mystery or detective story to have taken place. For example: A BUTLER in a ZOO used a LASER BEAM because of LOVE to commit a crime, and so the story goes from there. With the plot chart, thousands of combinations are possible.

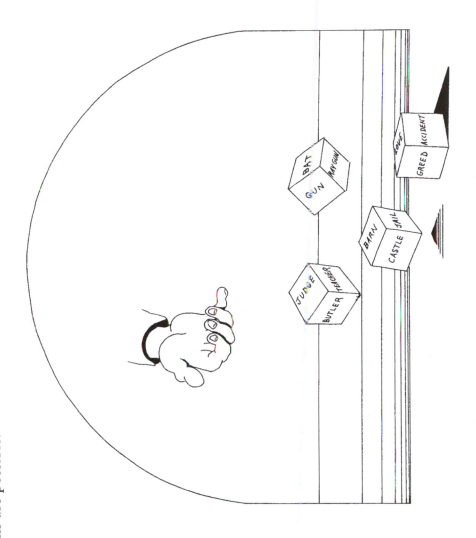

The other way to accomplish the same thing is to make "plot dice." Put the story elements on wooden dice cut from a piece of 2" × 2" lumber. You need a minimum of four plot dice, one for each story element of character, setting, method, and motive. To obtain a set of story elements, the student throws each of the plot dice and creates a story from the elements that turn up.

The plot dice are more restrictive than the plot chart because you can get only six characters, settings, and so forth, on each die, whereas the plot chart has fifty-one possible choices in the character section alone.

Creative writing is an important part of any English program. Communication skills are becoming increasingly important as expanding technology shrinks this globe. The plot chart or the plot dice will give your students a "jump start" in the art of writing.

204

Figure 4-2

CREATIVE WRITING PLOT CHART

Choose a person and a setting (location) and combine these with a modus operandi (method) and a motive (reason) to help you develop your creative story.

Person	judge, doctor, lawyer, detective, maid, butler, teacher, teenager, sailor, soldier, spy, thief, principal, mother, father, druggist, rogue, king, queen, janitor, trucker, cowboy, nurse, patient, taxi driver, model, farmer, movie maker, mechanic, pilot, crime boss, slave, flight attendant, CIA agent, president, announcer, show host, smuggler, bus driver, friend, jogger, lion tamer, vice president, scoundrel, boxer, wrestler, robot, alien, dentist, professor, veterinarian
Setting	At a(n) . . . post office, desert, barn, club, classroom, sewer, air, ocean, farm, city, suburbs, jungle, mountains, castle, dungeon, school, jail, back yard, house, store, airplane, boat, car, car lot, pig sty, movie lot, office, construction site, launch pad, living room, basement, outer space, zoo, garage, stage, trailer, street, downtown, graveyard, open field, inside a video machine, mall, swimming pool, race track, video arcade, ball diamond, football field, gun club, diamond mine, foreign country
Modus Operandi	Use (a) . . . poison, suffocation, gun, knife, run over, blow gun, bow and arrow, sling shot, rope, rifle, machine gun, spear, tank, grenade, speeding truck (car), fighter jet, cruise missile, thermonuclear device, blasting cap, laser beam, pea shooter, firecracker, dynamite, smoke, fire, pollution, ray gun, baseball bat, spear gun, spit ball, paint ball gun, radar beam
Motive	Because (of) . . . love, revenge, greed, hate, principle, money, passion, accident, no reason, enjoyment, mistake, for the fun of it, insanity, drunkenness, drugs, fear, no fear, it seemed like a good idea at the time, a lust for power, mind control, an experiment, thrills, punishment, gluttony, hallucination, optical illusions, luck, tiredness, anger, sloth, organized crime, covetousness, pride, envy

VOLUNTEERS—WONDERFUL HELPERS

Every school could use extra help for those thousand and two tasks that seem to be pressing continuously. This problem seems to multiply itself if you want to have extra or special programs or events at the school. Many people are willing to help. While some may have to be trained (e.g., how to use the photocopier), others are, or have been, professionals in their lives and will take to the extra tasks around the school in a creative and competent manner.

Having volunteers around the school can be a wonderful thing; however, there are some pitfalls and areas that should be considered when allowing volunteers to come into your school.

SOME GUIDELINES

1. Check your school board policy in this area before going ahead. There may be a rigid set of procedures to follow.

2. Parents are the greatest pool from which to draw volunteers. This is not the only group that will help you, however. Retired teachers are often willing to fulfill this role, as are many retired professionals from other skill areas.

3. There must be some restriction as to what information (e.g., student marks) is made available to the volunteer. The volunteer should understand that the school rules apply to all persons in the school, including him or her.

4. Top on the list of instructions to the volunteer should be the fact that the confidentiality of teachers and students must be respected. To this end, the volunteer should read and sign the Volunteer Contract (Figure 4-3) provided for this purpose. This helps ensure that the rights of everyone are protected.

5. Under no circumstances is the volunteer to be seen as filling the role of a teacher aide or janitor, or in any way eliminating or reducing the employment of any person.

6. There must, of course, be some screening of volunteers. Persons with known criminal backgrounds or unstable personalities should not be in the school. Develop a set of practical criteria for screening volunteers.

7. Keep a log of volunteer hours—who has worked where and when. This enables administration to provide recognition for volunteer work at year end. In the event of a problem, you have documentation of which volunteer worked where and when. The Volunteer Log Sheet (Figure 4-4) is provided for this purpose.

206

Figure 4-3

VOLUNTEER CONTRACT

I, _____, am volunteering to

work at _____ School on _____ days and

at _____ times of the day.

I have been informed of the school rules or procedures, and I will abide by

them. I will respect the rights of the students and staff as to confidentiality in the

education process.

_____
Signature of Volunteer

_____
Principal or Vice-Principal

Figure 4-4

VOLUNTEER LOG SHEET

NAME	DATE	AREA OF WORK	TEACHER/SUPERVISOR

102

THE POINT TARGET SHEET

The Quick, Efficient Essay Grading System

One of the major problem areas for teachers is the physical process of correcting papers. There are many types of tests or evaluations that allow easy correcting. These include short-answer, fill-in-the-blanks, and true-or-false tests. These tests work well and have their place, but some subjects do not lend themselves to these easily corrected formats. Some subjects require essays, reports, or essay-type tests to facilitate a comprehensive evaluation.

How do you efficiently and quickly grade those thirty-two essays or essay-type test answers you brought home tonight? How can you read them to pick out the exact details you are looking for and not miss a point or two? Some students will write at great length and not put down the information you are looking for. How do you make sure quantity does not become a substitute for quality?

The most efficient way to grade an essay or essay-type test is to develop a Point Target Sheet for each essay (see the Sample Point Target Sheet, Figure 4-5). This sheet lists all the points or bits of information you want the students to have in place as they write out the essay or answers to the essay questions.

When you read the student's work, you mark the score on the Point Target Sheet, not on the essay or essay answers of the student. On the sheet, you may simply put a check mark on each point as you come across it in your reading, or you may desire to write a percentage after each point.

The Point Target Sheet will also allow you to look at the mechanics of the essay itself and grade this as "process." The Sample Point Target Sheet was developed to target answers to the following essay question: Describe the life and times of George Washington before his military career.

209

Figure 4-5

Sample Point Target Sheet

Date: _____

Essay Question: Describe the life and times of George Washington before his
                   military career.

Process: 10%

Proper Sentences _____, Spelling _____, Punctuation _____,
Neatness _____ Evidence of Effort _____, Followed Instruction _____,
Met Due Date _____, Proper Paragraphs _____, Attractiveness _____,
Rough Copy Attached _____

* *

Target Points each worth 3%

1. Family name in England, de Wessington
2. Believed in hard work
3. Family had strong faith in God
4. Father's name, Augustine Washington
5. Mother's maiden name, Mary Ball
6. George born Pope's Creek Farm, VA
7. Moved to Mount Vernon at age 3
8. In 1738, father buys farm on Rappahannock River
9. Has only 7 or 8 years of schooling
10. Strong math student
11. Father dies, George age 11
12. Ends schooling at age 14 or 15
13. Develops lifelong love for horses
14. Becomes an expert dancer
15. As a young man is sober, quiet and alert
16. Strong and patient through problems
17. George greatly admires and emulates older half brother Lawrence
18. Mother will not let George join British Navy
19. Surveys for Lord Fairfax
20. Surveys for town of Alexandria, VA
21. Appointed surveyor for Culpeper County
22. Surveys Shenandoah Valley
23. Keeps excellent financial records
24. By end of 1750, he owns 1500 acres
25. Travels to Barbados in 1751
26. Studies Barbados farming methods
27. Contracts smallpox in West Indies
28. Returns to Virginia after recovery
29. Falls in love with Betsy Fauntleroy
30. At age 20 seeks military career

Total _____

103

THE VALUE OF CPR AND FIRST-AID TRAINING FOR TEACHERS

The value of CPR and first-aid training for teachers is beyond measure; no value can be placed on the life of a child or colleague you save. There is no more helpless feeling than to be in a crisis situation and not know what to do.

In one case, an eleven-year-old boy was participating in a track and field day at a local elementary school when, without warning, he went into cardiac arrest on the track, right in front of several teachers, parents, and other students. No one knew what to do and panic ensued. The child was already turning blue when the physical education teacher, some distance away at the high jump, saw the commotion and came running. Fortunately, he had taken CPR training eight months earlier. He immediately took over, and with a sustained effort, was able to revive the child. He got the boy's heart beating again, and color and consciousness returned just as the ambulance arrived. The boy eventually became a strong, functioning student once again.

Had that teacher not had CPR training, the results most likely would have been quite different. That physical education instructor is truly a teacher hero because of CPR.

CPR and first-aid training for teachers is essential because of the continuous contact teachers have with many people each day. The number of students and others with whom teachers are associated increases the likelihood of encountering a problem requiring an emergency response.

GUIDELINES TO REMEMBER

1. Cardiopulmonary resuscitation (CPR) is clearly defined as an emergency external first-aid technique that uses outside compression to maintain respiration and blood circulation to a patient whose heart has stopped.

2. The brain begins to be permanently damaged or to die about four minutes after breathing has stopped.

3. Perform first aid only up to your level of competence; enlist help or advice as soon as possible. Only persons trained in CPR should attempt to perform it.

4. If a problem does occur at school, and a student is severely injured or dies—and CPR or quality first aid was not performed—the courts may raise this as an issue for litigation.

5. Knowledge of how to use the Heimlich maneuver is of prime importance for school staff. Students or staff can choke on the simplest and most surprising things.

6. CPR and first-aid courses are available from the American Heart Association, the American Red Cross, and many local hospitals and community schools.

7. In some cases, CPR courses do not include first-aid training; however, most first-aid courses contain CPR training. Check this out before purchasing an in-service package.

8. School staff should undergo upgrading or recertification for first-aid and CPR techniques at least once every three years. Skills get rusty, and in a three-year span, school staff can change substantially.

211

104

THE NOTEBOOK CHECK AND GRADE SHEET

Many teachers grade or evaluate student notebooks; it is an excellent way to judge whether the student has completed the required day-to-day tasks.

By what criteria do you grade the notebook? The Notebook Check and Grade Sheet (Figure 4-6) is the answer. It allows for a rating to be affixed to four critical areas:

1. Completion of assignments to date.

2. Degree of neatness.

3. Extent to which corrections have been completed, if applicable.

4. The overall quality of notebook organization.

If students know a notebook will be evaluated at certain intervals, they are more likely to maintain their notebooks at a proper level. A check of the notebooks reveals whether students have the necessary board notes and other data that will be required for any upcoming tests, reports, or essays.

THREE NOTES

1. Photocopy a different sheet for each student, and a different sheet for each subject area.

2. How you use the rating scale is up to you. You may want to convert it to a percentage, or simply leave it as it is.

3. Normally, the teacher keeps the main copy of the notebook check and grade sheet. A photocopy of the sheet should be given to the student as part of the feedback from evaluation.

Figure 4-6

NOTEBOOK CHECK AND GRADE SHEET

Name: _____   Grade _____

1. Extent of assignments completed to date   /10

2. Degree of neatness   /10

3. Extent to which corrections have been performed   /10

4. Quality of organization   /10

                                                        Total   /40

NOTEBOOK CHECK AND GRADE SHEET

Name: _____   Grade _____

1. Extent of assignments completed to date   /10

2. Degree of neatness   /10

3. Extent to which corrections have been performed   /10

4. Quality of organization   /10

                                                        Total   /40

105

PORTFOLIOS OR DOCUMENT FOLDERS

It is important to have discipline over the organizational problems that plague every classroom. Many students, because of their immaturity or lack of training, tend to have their learning materials scattered from the classroom to Timbuktu. This becomes a problem for you when you must refer to a particular item or piece of work.

One very good way to help keep students' work organized is to have them develop portfolios or document folders in which to keep their work. These folders are especially important in this day of multi-resource-based learning, when not all learning tools fit neatly into a three-ring binder.

SOME FUNCTIONAL IDEAS

1. The portfolios or document folders should be constructed out of lightweight cardboard that is at least as strong as the grade used for file folders. The average professional-sized portfolio is 12 inches (30 cm) high by 18 inches (46 cm) wide. This is folded to make the portfolio 12 inches (30 cm) by 9 inches (23 cm). See the diagram on p.215.

2. The portfolio should be stored in the student's locker or storage area each day when work is finished. Completed or full portfolios should be placed in secure storage for future reference or taken home.

3. Usually, these document folders are used for one school term and then recycled for the next term.

4. Document folders or portfolios are great for parent-teacher conferences. Everything is easily laid out before parents as you open a student's folder.

5. All material in the portfolios should be dated so students, parents, and teachers can see a progression of the work.

6. Students can personalize the folders with their own art.

7. How you use the document folders or portfolios in terms of time, space, and work quantity is at your discretion; however, it is usually most convenient to have only one portfolio per subject per term. This allows students to fit most materials into their portfolios without the folders themselves becoming unmanageable.

8. The following items can be included in the average portfolio or document folder:

- computer disks
- surveys
- leaf collections
- graded tests
- photographs
- audiocassettes
- art

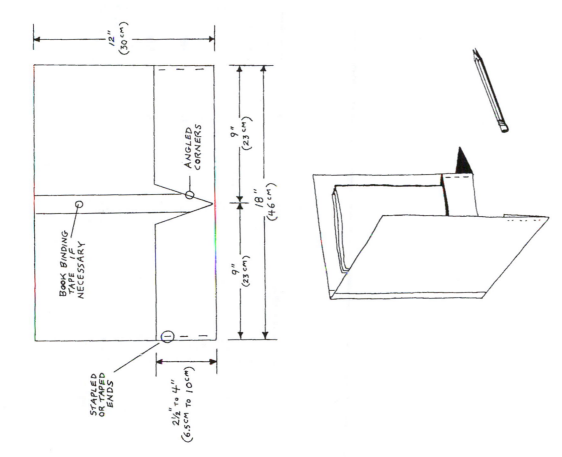

12"
(30 cm)

9"
(23 cm)

18"
(46 cm)

9"
(23 cm)

ANGLED CORNERS

BOOK BINDING TAPE IF NECESSARY

STAPLED OR TAPED ENDS

2½" TO 4"
(6.5 cm TO 10 cm)

↟ worksheets

↟ tables and charts

↟ personal notes on the subject area

↟ assignments to be completed

↟ graphic displays

↟ board notes

↟ reports

↟ essays

↟ letters to and from pen friends

↟ research papers

↟ computer printouts

215

106

PROTECT YOURSELF—READ THIS

One of the most important realities you must face in the world of teaching today is that you may be taken to court as part of a litigation process. You can become part of a lawsuit due to some incident that happened at school, and that incident does not have to be current. In many jurisdictions, you can be sued or face litigation until the statute of limitations runs out in the case. The statute varies from state to state; in one state, it may say that the case can be opened only until the student initiating the case reaches the age of majority, and in another state, it may have a specific time limit. That time limit has been known to be as long as twenty years.

One further problem that exists with lawsuits is that when people register the lawsuit, they name all persons—even those remotely involved with the perceived problem for which they want redress. This is called the *scatter effect*. If you suspect a problem, definitely consult your teachers' federation or union for advice.

What else can you do right now to protect yourself from the specter of a lawsuit arising from an incident at school? Keep accurate, consistent records on an Incident Flowchart (Figure 4-7). This way of documenting an incident will give you the best credibility if you are challenged in court.

Every record-keeping system will come under scrutiny in a court of law. The Incident Flowchart is no different; it therefore must be adapted to legal situations in your state. What the Incident Flowchart does is give you a frame of reference to understand what should be documented and how.

SEVEN RULES THAT APPLY TO ANY FLOWCHART

1. Write everything down in pen and ink; do not use erasable pen or pencil.

2. Do not use liquid typewriter or ink eraser for errors.

3. Do not cover any writing with black marker.

4. When an error occurs, run a line through it and initial the error.

5. Draw a line under the last part of an entry, so no one can add anything. This line also shows that you did not fill it in as a last-minute measure before the litigation (if entries of other incidents follow it).

6. Lock up the binder that contains your Incident Flowcharts.

7. Keep old Incident Flowcharts in storage for at least twenty years.

In many cases, when an Incident Flowchart is used consistently by staff members of a school or school system, it has more credibility and therefore is more likely to hold up in the courts.

Protect yourself; the trauma, personal grief, and anxiety that arise from a lawsuit—and the resulting legal ramifications—can deeply hurt you personally and professionally, even if you and any colleagues you may be supporting are completely innocent.

Figure 4-7

INCIDENT FLOWCHART

Date Y/M/D	Time	Place	Persons Involved	What Provoked the Incident	Description of Incident	Witness	Intervention Taken	Persons Notified	Signature

THE COMMUNITY SERVICE PROGRAM

One of the most difficult concepts to teach is the idea of having a genuine, unselfish care or concern for other people. It is important for students to see value in the lives of people around them, and to develop a sense of real care and compassion for others less fortunate than themselves. One program that has met with a great deal of success is the community service program. In this kind of program, students are given a series of choices for doing community service in an area that involves a substantial amount of personal relating and interaction.

Identify and locate those places that would benefit from an extra pair of hands or a good listening ear. A seniors' nursing or retirement home and a school for the emotionally or physically disabled offer two examples of places that always need an extra hand or other caring help.

A list of places that would welcome volunteers should be available from a social service agency or mental health association.

GUIDELINES

1. Students must receive some training on the behavior of the clients of the placement location and on how to treat these people respectfully. This instruction should be given to the students by a staff member of the placement location.

2. Students typically go to the community service placement once a week for two to three hours over a two-month period at each location.

3. A teacher/supervisor is required for this program. This person circulates from one placement location to another at the time the students are serving at the designated location.

4. Try to match the personalities of students to the job placement locations. This would, of necessity, be a judgment call on the part of the teacher/supervisor.

5. Definite roles or behavior guidelines (especially in the area of theft) must be given to the students. Students must be totally honest and not self-seeking.

6. The students are in no way to replace the regular employees of the placement location.

7. The community service program should be rotational, with the students transferring to at least three placements each school year.

8. Students are to interact with the residents or clients of the nursing home, rehabilitation center, or other location. Their duties might include visiting, reading to the residents, playing cards, or assisting the recreational director with other games.

9. Whether the student is to receive credit for the class time spent on this program is at your discretion.

10. Students' tasks at the placement locations must be of a giving-for-no-return nature; there is, of course, no pay. Their rewards would come from responses of the residents and from performing unselfish tasks for others less fortunate.

The community service program has a major double benefit. First, the student is called upon to be helpful and altruistic at a time in his or her development when it is very meaningful. The people who are helped or befriended by the students really enjoy the young people; the vibrancy of youth is always refreshing. Many times, the feeling of unselfish caring or helping others translates into a more understanding, and therefore better, student in the school.

© 1998 by The Center for Applied Research in Education

218

HOW A CAMERA CAN ASSIST
IN THE DISCIPLINE AND PR PROCESS

Numerous management tools and ideas are available to facilitate different aspects of discipline in the classroom, as well as in the school at large. Some of those ideas work well and have stood the test of time; the use of a school camera is truly of this genre.

Not only is the school camera good for management purposes; it, of course, has the added feature of being the best PR tool in town. We will deal first with how the camera can be used to assist in the discipline process.

GUIDELINES

1. In some schools—and not only in the inner city—outside people have been seen selling drugs to students on playgrounds or engaging in other undesirable activities. A photograph of these outside people will aid in the prosecution process.

   A spin-off of the photograph idea is to have the school board erect a sign stating, "School yard and surroundings under 24-hour video surveillance." This, in itself, is a wonderful deterrent, even if you can't afford the video surveillance. Remember, the sign must be in plain view to avoid problems of entrapment and invasion of privacy.

2. If there is a rumor of a fight about to happen in the school yard, the presence of a camera around the school yard supervisor's neck will often stop the fight before it even begins. If the fight does take place, a good photograph of the participants and the spectators will be excellent for later disciplinary action.

3. The camera can implicate a person who is in possession of any type of weapon.

4. If a teacher, before receiving a new group of students, is able to study the pictures of the new pupils and go over the behavior of each child with the previous teacher of that group, then the new teacher will be better prepared for his or her incoming students. In addition, the teacher will be able to put names to faces much more easily.

5. Evidence of damage perpetrated by a student is more credible with a picture of the situation.

6. Occasionally, a teacher with a camera on supervision can photograph errant behavior (e.g., throwing rocks) while it is in progress—that is, if the teacher is not too busy putting a stop to the behavior in the first place!

HOW A CAMERA CAN BE USED FOR PR

1. Photograph the students at sports and other events and put these on display—then send these pictures home to the parents when new ones take their place.

2. Photograph visitors to the school and have a display wall for these VIPs.

3. Place pictures in the local paper on a regular basis (once a week, if possible). Make sure each picture is accompanied by a positive caption or uplifting story.

THE ANECDOTAL PROTECTION SYSTEM

In our culture, teachers see the problems of child abuse, neglect, and social dysfunctions of all sorts. The results of those problems are becoming manifest in our classrooms. Increasingly, teachers are called upon as witnesses in court cases that deal with these problems.

How can you, as a teacher, keep a record of circumstances that may or may not be a major component in an abuse or divorce proceeding? How can you keep a record of the daily routine that does not bog you down with a great deal of paperwork?

One of the best ways to manage this problem is to keep a binder of the Anecdotal Record Forms in your desk (Figure 4-8). This form allows you to write the three most necessary pieces of information as preparation for these cases. They are:

1. What you observed.

2. What the child said about it.

3. What was done about it (by you or others).

When you observe some situation, such as a student crying for no apparent reason, you first resolve the problem, then fill in the form. Stamp or write in the date. Once the Anecdotal Record Form is filled in, place it in the special binder you keep for this purpose.

It is not necessary to fill in a form for each student each day. The logistics of this would soon become overwhelming. Once you have worked with a class for a few days, you will be able to determine which students are in need of this attention and which ones are not.

What you have created is a professional-looking, anecdotal record of the anomalies associated with the children in your class. Needless to say, because of the sensitive nature of such information, it is imperative that confidentiality be maintained and the student be protected. *The binder should be kept under strict lock and key at all times.*

In the event you are asked to describe the behavior or circumstance of a student by school officials or in a court proceeding, you will have a solid record of any problems that exist at that time, or did exist some time ago. Otherwise, it is difficult to remember off the top of your head what a student said or how he or she looked four or five months—or even two years—in the past.

This type of anecdotal record system has been presented in court and accepted as valid by the participants in the litigation.

Figure 4-8

ANECDOTAL RECORD FORM

Name: _____   Date: _____

1. What was observed:

_____

_____

_____

2. What the student said about it: _____

_____

_____

3. What was done about it: _____

_____

_____

_____
Teacher Signature

110

THE PARADIGM EXPANSION CHART

Some ideas in teaching are worth their weight in gold as far as creating effective communication is concerned. The Paradigm Expansion Chart is one of these.

This chart (Figure 4-9) is a great mechanism for starting discussions and focusing students on a topic, as it expands the point of view or paradigm. The chart is especially valuable when discussing an abstract concept like "tolerance," for example. Some students tend to be concrete in their thinking, and it is here that the Paradigm Expansion Chart really shines. It draws the students working on the topic out of themselves and gives others new ideas as they brainstorm.

How to Use It

1. Separate the students into workable groups of three or four.

2. Present each group with a Paradigm Expansion Chart on which you have written the concept under discussion.

3. On the chart, the students as a group fill in items for each heading on the chart. A minimum of four ideas should be written for each heading.

4. After the chart is filled in and the concepts developed, it is best to appoint a spokesperson for the group to report its findings to the class.

Included here is an example of what a chart should look like once students have filled in four items for each heading.

Topic: Tolerance

What does it look like?	What does it feel like?	What does it sound like?
smiles not frowns	hand shake	"Greetings one and all."
eye contact	pat on the back	"Yes, I agree."
positive body language	helping hand	"You are forgiven."
mixed-group involvement	working together	"We are all equal."

Figure 4-9

THE PARADIGM EXPANSION CHART

TOPIC _____

INDIVIDUAL OR GROUP MEMBERS _____

What does it look like?	What does it feel like?	What does it sound like?

111

THE CUSTODIAL STAFF—
PROBLEM SOLVERS FOR YOU

In any school, you have people who look after the absolutely necessary janitorial duties. The running of the physical plant of the school requires a fair amount of expertise, and many of these people are required to have a professional maintenance or firefighter's certificate in order to qualify for such a position.

Some teachers only see the custodian sweeping floors or washing windows—their connection ends there. In fact, the janitor is one of the best allies in your teaching day. He or she is a key player in the education of the students in the school.

The custodian or janitor must not only possess the skills to keep the heating and electrical system of the school in top shape; this person must have well-developed repair skills. Whether it is fixing furniture, locating extra desks, or repairing the old fish tank in the corner, the janitor can be a tremendous help with the thousand and one things you must accomplish in the normal school year or term.

If you develop a positive working relationship with this staff member, you will find that he or she will go the extra mile to help you, especially in times of emergency or when you have a special request—for example, when you need geranium pots for a seed project.

Use these helpful hints for getting along with the custodial staff:

1. Introduce yourself to the janitor as soon as possible. Get to know this person on a first-name, friendly basis.

2. It helps if the principal makes a regular habit of having coffee or tea with these workers in the maintenance office. At informal times like these, bonds of trust are developed and insights are exchanged.

3. The janitor should be invited to use the staff lounge or staff room, along with all other staff members.

4. Every school should promote a Janitor Appreciation Day, when all the staff and students are made aware of the contribution the maintenance people make to the school.

5. You can help the janitor in his or her daily routine by having the students tidy up the classroom at the end of each school day.

6. In some schools, the members of the janitorial staff are subjected to a great many demands for repairs and other help. To avoid overwhelming the maintenance people, who also have routine duties to attend to, the best approach is to have the requests for work written on a requisition form. The work is then accomplished in chronological sequence, and no one feels slighted.

8. Adopt a no-gum, no-candy, no-junk-food policy for the whole school. It's a wonderful show of support for the custodial staff.

9. Many janitors have collections of lost pens and pencils. On occasion, they can be a good source of these items—especially when students "forget" to bring theirs to class.

A noted educator once said that the physical plant of the school in the twenty-first century would have to be a "culture of maintenance." This is especially true with tight budgets and dwindling resources, combined with ever-increasing demands.

A good, top-notch maintenance person with diverse repair skills can save the school thousands of dollars that can be effectively used elsewhere. A good janitor is one of the most valuable assets a school can have.

225

Section Five

SPEAK EASY—
THE COMMUNICATION SECTION

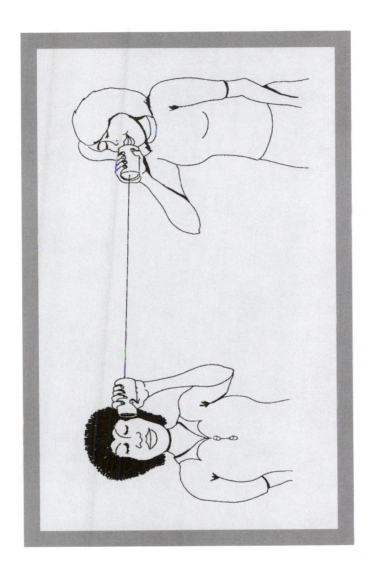

Communication is the name of the game in teaching. A wonderful teacher is a wonderful communicator.

Some people are born with dynamic skills in communication, but for most of us, it is a learned set of approaches, methods, and techniques. Many of the communication tools offered in this section will help you maintain a positive rapport not only with your students but with the parents of those students as well.

This last section abounds with highly effective communication ideas. The Missed-Assignment Binder is a classic example; if you use this idea, students can never say they missed getting the required instructions to do an assignment.

Good communication skills not only help you speak more easily, they help you write and listen better, thereby making your work just that much more satisfying each day.

Delivery skills and insights in all areas of communication are vital to an effective teacher or administrator. The fifty communication tips offered here will strengthen your communication proficiency when you interact with students.

1. Communicate with the families of your students before school begins. In a letter, make your new students feel welcome as you introduce yourself. In this way, you are setting a positive tone for the rest of the school year.

2. Principals and vice-principals must be able to communicate positive reinforcement to all school staff members as well as to the students.

3. Remember, if a student argues with you, he or she has the problem—and probably argues with other teachers and his or her parents as well.

4. Always place notices of reports, essays, and assignments due in a conspicuous location in the classroom.

5. You communicate by how you dress. You don't have to be the "isle of style," but if you dress in an odd manner, you are setting yourself up for ridicule, which hurts your credibility.

6. Anger is not a communication skill.

7. Use a pointer wherever it will help the students to focus on what you are talking about.

8. If a student is speaking to you from a crowd of highly verbal children, point at that student, so he or she knows you are focused on him or her.

9. You sometimes communicate more by what you do and what you are than by what you say. (Actions speak louder than words.)

10. Seek out and use humor to enrich your teaching presentations. One-line jokes are great, for example—Q: What do you give a sick bird? A: Tweetment.

11. If it suits your style in the classroom, develop the running joke. You can do this if you have a situation with a student or students that you can refer to many times during the school year. (Example: One day Myron challenged me to an arm wrestle. Now, I'm built like a sumo wrestler, and Myron might be all of 95 pounds. I let him try to move my arm, which he couldn't budge an inch. For days and weeks afterward, when I saw Myron, I complained, "Hey! My arm sure is sore, Myron," or "Gee, Myron, what kind of power did you have? The agony is always with me." Everyone knew Myron had no effect on me, and he didn't move my arm or hurt me at all, but he enjoys the banter and the fact that I gave him a touch of "power.") The running joke is effective because it sets a light, positive mood for the class. It can, however, get stale after awhile, so be aware of the need to end it.

12. If you are assertive in your communication, you will have greater control over the environment of your classroom.

229

13. If you accidentally put down a student, instantly apologize and continue teaching; do not make an issue of it.

14. When you speak to students, focus on success rather than failure.

15. You must have the self-discipline not to swear or curse when the students are within earshot.

16. School notices for the students should be placed in a convenient spot in the hall on a white board that requires the use of markers. This board is less likely than a regular chalkboard to have a message erased from it.

17. Your school visitor and security policy should be in an easy-to-read location near the entrance of the school.

18. If a student has difficulty writing the circumstances of a problem, have him or her draw a picture of the problem instead. Then, ask the student to describe the picture either verbally or in writing.

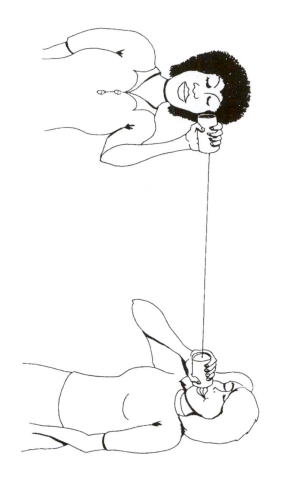

19. Update the mark status of each student every two weeks if you give a lot of assignments. Students need to know where they are.

20. Communication with parents should be as open as possible.

21. Not all communication is verbal. A large percentage of what you say is a function of body language. Negative body language will strongly detract from the impact of your presentation.

22. When presenting a topic or to emphasize a point, repeat it about one or two decibels louder. This is a common technique used by public speakers who want their audience to pay direct attention to the main idea.

23. Watch out for the "I Can'ter" and the "I Don'ter" at staff meetings. Perfectly wonderful ideas have been tossed out by someone who said, "I can't do that" or "I don't do this." These people are at the tail end of progress.

230

24. Hone your feedback skills. When you are explaining a concept in math, for example, watch the eyes and the facial expressions of the students. You will soon be able to tell whether they understand how to do the work.

Many times, when you ask the student if he or she understood the data, the student will say "Yes" in muted tones—not wanting to appear dumb—yet still have that vague, faraway look on his or her face. At this point, you must repeat the instructions, because the student did not internalize the information.

25. Many schools have a policy (written or not) whereby you are not allowed to present your religious beliefs. It should also hold true that those with no religious belief system should exercise professional politesse, and not denigrate religious beliefs of anyone else, either overtly or subtly.

26. Brainstorming is an expansion of communication technique. The basic rules are:

⬆ You need a topic that can be worked on in this way.

⬆ The expansion can occur with as few as two people participating.

⬆ The sessions exist to produce a quantity of ideas.

⬆ There are to be no value judgments (e.g., What a dumb idea!) by anyone about any idea.

⬆ Participants are to stay on the topic.

⬆ Ideas are to expand upon one another like popcorn flying out of the popper.

⬆ Different or unusual ideas are to be fostered and encouraged.

27. Watch for your right or left dominance when making a presentation to the class. Make sure you don't favor or focus your attention on one side or the other.

28. If it is necessary to have a student repeat a grade, inform the student and the parents before the report cards are given out. It may be advisable to allow the repeating child to pick up his or her report card on a day other than when they are given out to the other students. Avoid using the word FAILURE!

29. Communicate with—teach—students so they will learn and grow in knowledge. Do not teach to a test.

30. Listening is sometimes your best form of communication. This is why you have two ears and only one mouth.

31. Be aware at all times that, in the course of a disagreement, voices tend to rise in one or both of the participants. Voices can soar to the point of yelling. When this occurs, there is no longer effective communication.

32. When you make a presentation to a new class or a group of teachers, it will take a minimum of seven to twelve minutes for them to warm up to you, no matter how humorous or likable you are. It will take that long for them to adjust to your style and come to the conclusion that you are not threatening.

33. Use the expression, "Hey! That's a good question!" when a student asks one on the topic you are teaching. Say it even if the question, in your eyes, is "iffy" at best. This one-line statement rewards the student for asking a question, and that is what you should be encouraging.

34. You can communicate by how you adorn your classroom. A well-decorated classroom with bright, cheery posters, colorful designs, and mobiles will convey a positive feel to anyone entering your learning environment.

35. If you are caught in a confrontation, you can gain control over the situation only if you ask the other person(s) questions that require responses.

36. If another teacher needs you to cover or look after a class for him or her on your free or spare period, do so cheerfully. Make sure that you in no way communicate that you are reluctant or do not want to cover that person's class. You never know when you will need the favor returned.

37. Do not begin a presentation by being self-effacing. You will hurt the credibility of your presentation if you run yourself down.

38. Encourage parents at an early parent-teacher conference to inform you and the school office of any physical or emotional problems they know of. This is especially important for children entering kindergarten or grade 1, where there is no history at the school on the child.

39. In order to maximize communication at parent-teacher conferences, ask the parents to bring a notepad or writing paper to the interview or conference. This will allow them to record accurately what was discussed.

40. One of the worst communication insults occurs when one of the parties to a discussion looks away during the conversation. The person looking aside gives the impression that he or she does not care about the other person or the topic, even if the words used say he or she does. Excuse yourself if you must look away, for example, for supervision.

41. Be alert in the normal teaching interaction with students to the possibility that they will try to get you off the topic. Many times students will ask about what personally concerns you. They will talk about the cars you like, the new coat you bought, or whether you voted in the last election; in short, they will talk about anything but the math or science lesson that you intended to teach.

42. When a student makes an error, send that student the "You're still okay" message.

43. Many teachers present a lesson with a good deal of repetition of concepts, and then give a related assignment. It is also a good idea to repeat instructions once again about one third of the way into the time when the students are actually doing the assignment. The intricacies and variations of a subject like algebra almost demand this.

44. Never forget when you are communicating with a parent about his or her child that it is almost impossible for that parent to be *truly* objective about his or her boy or girl.

45. If a parent complains about another child in the same classroom as his or her child, check to see if the two children are related before you go any further with the complaint.

232

46. It is sometimes a good idea to mail a photocopy of a student's school performance to the home, as well as to give the child a copy when the report cards are given out.

47. A school newspaper can be an effective communication device; however, the value must be weighed in terms of cost, education value, and teacher workload.

48. As a rule, schools should produce a school newsletter that is mailed to the parents. This letter can be a strong PR tool. It will keep parents aware of dates and times of events and happenings around the school. Parents like open communication and will get a better "feel" for the environment their children are in. This newsletter will lessen your reliance on the students to ensure that notices and other communications make it home.

49. One of the key areas where communication breaks down in school systems is between feeder and receiver schools (e.g., elementary to junior high).

    The curriculum may be designed to have a consistent flow of information; however, in the real world, different teachers emphasize different areas of the curriculum. It is important, therefore, to hold communication meetings each year, to discuss the content and stresses of the curriculum as students move from one school to another.

50. At the end of a school year, it is a wise idea to communicate with yourself for the following school year. Some of those notes could include:

    ➡ Insights that will help you deal with any upcoming problems.

    ➡ Knowledge of any resources that will become available in the new year.

    ➡ Combinations of locks or computer passwords that you might forget over the break.

    ➡ Messages about any unresolved situations that occurred at the end of the school year.

    ➡ Tentative plans for a new—and just great—school year.

233

THE CLASS DIARY

It can truly be said that today's classroom is a busy place. In that classroom, the teacher is the center of a barrage of questions, demands, and requirements for decision making while satisfying each and every student's educational needs.

The amount of social interaction that goes on in the average school classroom of twenty-eight to forty students would boggle the mind of people in many other professions. On these hectic days, you are constantly trying to educate, console, arbitrate, and organize your charges—and somehow have some room for your own personal needs.

Many people—parents, administrators, social workers, counselors—want reports, report cards, anecdotal records, and the like. Even the little nuances become important if you have a child in your class with some special problems (e.g., anaphylactic reactions). How do you keep track of it all? While it would be impossible and unnecessary to record everything, there is always enough of importance occurring each day for you to keep track of.

One of the best record keepers of all is the Class Diary Form (Figure 5-1). This easy-to-use tool utilizes the diary form to help you keep track of the flow in the classroom in the most efficient manner possible. Each form is good for two consecutive days. It is often best to jot notes in the diary as the day progresses; you can expand on them later. In any event, if you are called upon to have some data from past events, or if there is a need for a chronological history of factors affecting a child, you will have it where and when you need it in the Class Diary.

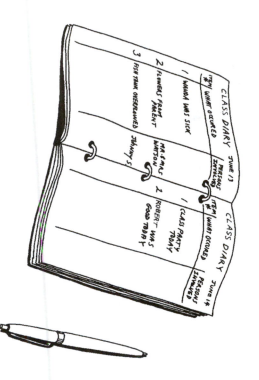

Figure 5-1
CLASS DIARY FORM

DATE: _____

ITEM #	WHAT OCCURRED	PERSONS INVOLVED
1		
2		
3		
4		
5		
6		
7		
8		

DATE: _____

ITEM #	WHAT OCCURRED	PERSONS INVOLVED
1		
2		
3		
4		
5		
6		
7		
8		

The technique offered here is best suited to rural schools or schools where there is a great deal of busing or parent pickup of students. Additionally, it is useful where there is a more-than-usual amount of interaction during the day between students and parents or people in the community.

This interaction is often necessary because of chores to be done, changes in pick-up times, or other information to be transmitted to the students. Parent communication with students in the classroom is often a sore spot for teachers. If a student is called to the door to receive a parental message, this disturbs the whole class. If this happens on a regular basis, the amount of disturbance will definitely cut into quality teaching time.

One technique to help cut down the number of times a class is disturbed is a mail-box system outside your classroom door. The mailboxes can be a formal set of boxes, nicely crafted by an industrial arts or wood shop student, or they can simply be a series of milk cartons adapted for this purpose.

Whenever there is a message to be given to a student, the message is placed in the student's mailbox outside the classroom. At the end of each period, or at recess or noon, the students check their mailbox for messages. This way, the class is not disturbed and students will learn the importance of the mail, and its need for security and privacy.

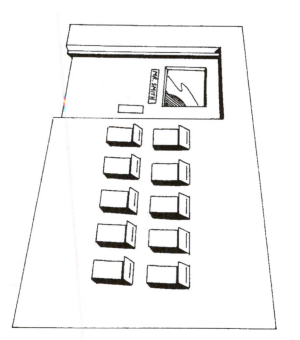

236

115 **ASSIGNMENT NOTEPADS**

You and your students are probably in need of some discipline over the ever-present necessity of keeping track of assignments, tests, and upcoming events. The idea presented here, if used properly, will allow students and parents to be better organized and aware of their daily responsibilities. This simple idea is to use small spiral notepads for each student to write assignments and other necessary information in.

SOME ADVANTAGES

1. The notepads are very inexpensive.

2. Students are to show their parents the notepads every night. A parent then signs or initials the bottom of each page that has an assignment on it.

   This, in itself, opens communication among parent, teacher, and student. Often, parents do not know what work is to be completed by their children; with this notepad, they will.

3. Parents will appreciate the routine. It shows that you and the students are progressing in order through the year.

4. Individual notes to parents can be written on a student's notepad, thus avoiding the need for phone calls.

➡ You will have to check the notepads consistently, to make sure they are serving the purpose for you.

116

TEACHER-TO-PARENT DATA COMMUNICATION FORM

We must have effective communication with the parents of our students. These parents want you to give them information that is concrete and meaningful. Normally, they are not interested in "theories of behavior modification" or "an analysis of cognitive processes" as it relates to their children. They want to know how well a daughter or son is performing at her or his ability level, and quite often, how well the child is performing in comparison with the rest of the class or the class average.

A very useful tool is the Teacher-to-Parent Data Communication Form (Figure 5-2). This form is designed to convey to parents exactly where their children are in terms of academic performance. It reveals the grade score of the student, the class average, the highest score in the class, the lowest score in the class, the number of assignments handed in by the student, and the attendance. These are the key areas affecting academic performance.

The numbers from 0 to 100 are printed around the perimeter of the form. This allows you to simply circle the grade score, class average, and so on, and draw a line to the appropriate area.

This tool is an excellent way for parents to see the academic progression of their children in your subject area. If you decide to supplement the report card with this form, you will find that parents have a much richer understanding of their children's performance as they progress through the school year.

Figure 5-2

TEACHER-TO-PARENT DATA COMMUNICATION FORM

Subject Area _____

0 100 99 98 97 96 95 94 93 92 91 90 89 88 87 86 85 84 83 82 81 80 79

1   78

2   77

3   76

4   Highest Score by a student   75

5   in the class   74

6   73

7   72

8   71

9   70

10 _____ Student Name   69

11   68

12   67

13   66

14   65

15   Days Attended   64

16   _____ out of _____   63

17   62

18   61

19   60

20   Lowest Score by a student   59

21   in the class   58

22   57

23   Number of Assignments   56

24   _____ handed in out of _____   55

25   54

26   53

27   52

28 29 30 31 32 33 34 35 36 37 38 39 40 41 42 43 44 45 46 47 48 49 50 51

117

THE MISSED-ASSIGNMENT BINDER

Many students will miss assignments when they have been absent for a day or more. These missed assignments can often be crucial in terms of grades or final marks.

How can you make sure students are aware of assignments they missed while they were not at school? An effective solution is to create a missed-assignment binder containing Missed-Assignment Sheets (Figure 5-3) for students to refer to when they return from absences. Teach the students to automatically look in the missed-assignment binder if they have been away for even one period.

Ideally, this binder should rest permanently on the corner of your desk. If you keep it in this location, you can easily reach the binder to record new assignments, and students will always know its exact location.

In this real world, where some students will not admit to having access to missed assignments, it is a good idea to have the students sign their names on the missed-assignment sheets that describe the work they missed. This way, you can quickly ascertain whether a student has read the assignment in the binder. A student signature on an assignment not eventually completed puts the responsibility squarely on the shoulders of the student—where it belongs.

Figure 5-3
MISSED-ASSIGNMENT SHEET

Description of Assignment and Directions _____

_____

_____

_____

_____

_____

_____

_____

Date Assigned _____   Date Due _____

Please sign below indicating you have read and understood the description and directions for the assignment.

1. _____ Date _____

2. _____ Date _____

3. _____ Date _____

4. _____ Date _____

5. _____ Date _____

6. _____ Date _____

7. _____ Date _____

8. _____ Date _____

9. _____ Date _____

10. _____ Date _____

118

ANOMIE—A TEACHER PROBLEM

Anomie—normlessness—is an acute problem for all teachers to some degree. The great paradox of teaching is that teachers continually give out positive reinforcement, but may receive little, if any, themselves.

As part of the human dynamic, teachers need to know they are doing a good job. It is highly unlikely that a student will come up to a teacher and sincerely say, "Thanks for the great algebra lesson today, Mr. Rodrigues." In other professions, there is usually some extraneous frame of reference. An optometrist, for example, will immediately realize that her or his patient sees better after treatment, and will often be directly thanked by the patient. This does not happen very often in teaching. The teacher, in many cases, has no feedback from anyone. A teacher does not often hear, "You did a good job today," or "I like what you created with this or that student." As a result of this lack of positive reinforcement, you may begin to ask the following questions: "Is what I am doing worthwhile?" or "Does anyone care?" Anomie can wear you down if you are not aware of its effects; it is one of the sources of burnout for new as well as long-term teachers and principals.

One way of combating the effects of such normlessness is to be your own reward system; set aside a notebook or even part of your day plan book to write, "This is what I did well today," and go on to describe the teachable moments or good things you accomplished for students or others on that particular day.

You can help break down the effects of anomie in your colleagues by sincerely telling them that you noticed some of the good things in their teaching program, or that you like the development of the skill level of particular students you work with now whom they had last year.

Schools run by an administrator who knows how to reward and reinforce the school staff tend to have a happier and more productive environment for the students. The staff will work harder for this person; there will be much less back-biting and fewer interpersonal squabbles. These things, in themselves, make for a smoother day at school. As Mark Twain said, "I can go two weeks on just one word of praise."

119

THE SIGN-OUT SHEET

Many teachers, by necessity, have to lend or assign to students materials, texts, and other equipment that must be returned to the teacher at some specific time. When any equipment is taken by a student, some form of record keeping is needed.

Ideally—if this were a perfect world, and all students returned everything assigned or borrowed by them by the due date—there would be no need to keep a record of materials lent out. However, things being far from perfect, a generic Sign-Out Sheet (Figure 5-4) is included here for your use.

When students know there is a correct, *signed* record of their borrowing equipment, they are much more likely to return it. Note that there is a space for the parent or guardian of the borrowing student to sign. In some jurisdictions, this is required.

Figure 5-4
SIGN-OUT SHEET

Student's Name: _____

Date Materials Assigned or Borrowed: _____   Teacher: _____

Return Due Date: _____

1. Description of Materials
    _____
    _____

2. Materials or Equipment Code _____

3. Condition of Materials or Equipment
    _____

4. Estimated Value of Materials or Equipment
    _____
    _____

5. Serial Number, if applicable _____

The student agrees:
(1) To borrow or be assigned the above described materials.
(2) To pay the estimated value of the materials or equipment if they are not returned by the return due date.
(3) To pay a portion of the estimated value if the materials or equipment are damaged or parts are missing. The value of the damaged or missing part is to be determined by the teacher.

_____   _____
Student Signature   Teacher Signature

_____
Parent/Guardian Signature

120 FOREIGN RELATIONS

Teachers are always looking for novel ideas for guest speakers as they seek to enrich and enhance the education of their students. The problem for history and social studies teachers is where to find that quality guest speaker who has experience with the culture of other lands. As a rule, there is no handy list of available people to draw from. The only way teachers sometimes find out about a good guest speaker is by the old, but unreliable, grapevine method. An additional drawback of this method is that a speaker can be overused or begin to charge a fee for this service.

How can you find a person from another culture who has reasonable English language skills, is low cost (if not free), and yet has a thorough knowledge of the country you currently have under study? The answer lies in the foreign student exchange programs that exist through many high schools and colleges. One phone call to the central office of a high school will get you the names of several students from other cultures. Another very good way to facilitate this is through the foreign student societies or clubs that exist on many college campuses today.

Because the person speaking to your class is usually young, a genuine rapport is established between the foreign student and your class of eager pupils. This is evidenced by the excellent and often insightful questions the students in your class will ask about the popular culture in the homeland of your guest. Many of these students have artifacts or symbols pertaining to the way of life in their home countries. This usually adds to the credibility of the speaker and stimulates great interest in the students.

One added positive note: Because the guest speaker has recently been in the school system of his or her home culture, he or she will often know the address of a school or schools at home. This is a great help when you want more information, or to develop pen friends with students from that other culture.

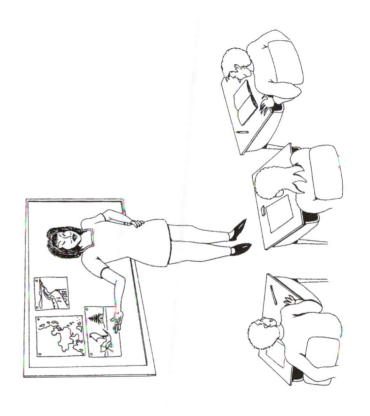

121

THE REPORT CARD MEMO

Many schools and school jurisdictions require that a report card memo be attached to the actual report card in cases where a student has not performed well academically, or when a student has some special circumstance or problem that affects the grade on the report card.

When you fill out a report card memo, it should be as detailed as possible. One-line comments, while they may be sufficient, do not allow for a detailed delivery of information.

There are many special circumstances that affect the education of children, and it is part of our duty to correctly inform parents of those positive or negative aspects. Such situations as lost class notes or a student's continual refusal to bring the proper materials to class can adversely affect a school grade.

While these situations may not have caused the student to fail the grade or class, they often result in the student's having obtained a lower mark than was possible. A well-written report card memo will often solve any communication problems between the teacher and parents on this.

The responsibility for the poor performance should be directed where it belongs—onto the student. The report card memo should indicate that all aspects of work and materials were made available to the student, and it is his or her responsibility to make good use of them in order to have good grades.

The Report Card Memo forms (Figures 5-5 and 5-6) included here have a space for the phone number of the school. This facilitates open communication with the parents should they want to discuss their children's performance any further. Chances are, you will not get a call from a parent if the report card memo you fill in is as detailed as possible.

Report card memos need not be used only for descriptions of problems or failures. Many students improve significantly or perform wonderfully in their academic skill areas. That improvement in grades or good work should be explained to the parents in equally detailed fashion at the time the report cards go out.

The two styles of report card memo have some degree of difference; one is more open for written comments and the other targets specific details or skill areas. This allows you to choose the report card memo form that best suits your situation.

Figure 5-5

REPORT CARD MEMO

Student's Name: _____

Date: _____

Class: _____

Teacher: _____

Subject(s): _____

School's Phone: _____

Test Scores: _____

Term Number: _____

* *

This memo is designed to inform you of the progress and performance of your child at school. Please contact the school if you have any concerns.

Teacher's Comments: _____

_____

_____

_____

_____

Recommendations: _____

_____

_____

_____

Teacher's Signature

Figure 5-6
REPORT CARD MEMO

Student's Name: _____

Class: _____   Date: _____

Subject(s): _____   Teacher: _____

Test Scores: _____   School's Phone: _____

                                           Term Number: _____

* *

The number beside each area indicates the level of performance.

(1) Excellent   (2) Good   (3) Satisfactory   (4) Needs Improvement   (5) Not Satisfactory

___ Working at ability level	___ Grade level scores
___ Degree of motivation	___ Homework
___ Regular attendance	___ Pays attention
___ Arrives at school on time	___ Gets along with peers
___ Arrives at class on time	___ Degree of cooperation
___ Attitude toward school work	___ Brings supplies to class

* *

Recommendations are checked ✓

___ Continue excellent work	___ Student needs to prepare for tests
___ Need improved overall effort	___ Student needs to improve in classroom
___ More attention needed on homework	___ Student needs to bring supplies to class
___ Behavior must improve	___ Parent/Teacher Conference required

Teacher Comments: _____

_____

_____

_____

Teacher Signature

122

THE PROS AND CONS OF ELEVEN DIFFERENT EVALUATION SYSTEMS

It is a given in the teaching profession that you must test or evaluate the students on the information you have taught them. The tests themselves are tools that are supposed to judge the degree to which students have learned the curriculum.

In the process of evaluation, some of the testing tools are in themselves limiting as to the amount and quality of responses needed in order to get a true picture of the amount of subject matter that has been internalized or learned by your students.

There are no perfect test or evaluation systems. Some teachers may swear by one type of test; however, an argument can be made for the viability of any test or assessment style. You must decide what is the best assessment or evaluation tool for your circumstance.

Here, is a look at the pros and cons of eleven different assessment devices or tools, as well as some test variables for you to consider.

VARIABLES

1. The test must meet the curriculum guidelines or requirements.

2. You must be aware of the time it will take to complete the test. Is one class period going to be sufficient?

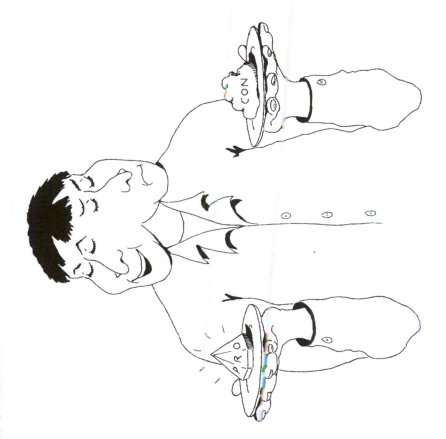

3. How can your test system best accommodate those students who are absent when the test is first given? It can take two weeks or more before everyone in the class is tested.

4. Do you feel it is necessary to provide some special accommodation for students who do poorly on tests (even though you know they have the knowledge) because of "test anxiety"?

5. What types of personalities are in this class? Some groups will lend themselves more easily to written or essay-type tests, rather than short-answer assessments.

6. Consider your school policies on testing.

Pro	Evaluation System	Con
Requires recall and comprehension Average preparation time Allows you to evaluate writing and grammar skills also Best used for English, hisotry, and similar subjects Best type of test to show students' total understanding of data Usually requires higher level of thinking skills	The Essay Test	Students may waste time on one question May require more than one period to complete Cannot easily be used for some subjects (math, trig.) Heavy reading or wading through data to get real answer Sometimes answer must be interpreted from information in context Usually results in a slower return of test results to students
Good for most subject areas Relies mainly on recognition Average to low prep time Easy to grade	Multiple Choice	Does not require high level of thinking skills Subject to guessing One of the least effective ways to assess learning
Easy to mark Quick return to students Light prep time	True or False	Subject to guessing One of the least effective ways to assess learning Not good for math, trig.

250

Table *(cont'd)*

Pro	Evaluation System	Con
Very comprehensive view of skills No prep time for tests per se Good for grading notebooks	Total Work Evaluation	Must wade through a volume of material Grade is assigned in a subjective manner No real, objective criteria
Quick response from student One must be prepared, but the examiner can draw out an answer by rephrasing a question Quick feedback to student	Verbal Test	Not much time to think over answers Body language can affect an answer Student may be affected by personality of examiner Verbal test presentation can be made to whole class but many will miss the gist of the question
Allows students to work with peers; helps promote cooperation Allows for brainstorming Good for history, social studies, and similar subjects	Project Evaluation (Group Grading)	Not good for math, trig. All in group must accept the same grade Does not reflect individual effort; one person may have done the bulk of the work and receive only the same grade as the others
More comprehensive because it requires a variety of skills Includes doing as well as thinking Average feedback time Can be continuous over the year Both subjective and objective evaluation	Up to 50% Participation Up to 50% Tests	An anecdotal record must be kept Much preparation needed
Will reflect a thorough knowledge of text and contents Reinforces learning of data as students prepare the answers	Open-Book Test	Students need a thorough knowledge of text as to where things are Need condensing and paraphrasing skills

Pro	Evaluation System	Con
The test itself becomes a reinforcer of subject data as students do research A vast amount of knowledge on topic areas can be accessed Low to average preparation time	Take-Home Test (The Research Test)	Students must have access to data base More difficult to grade because you must read a large amount of material
Easy to make Good for most grade levels Light prep time Requires recall Good for most subject areas	Fill in the Blanks	Answers can be obtained from context cues. Subject to guessing Only average in terms of effective evaluation
Behavior in class is good because of the need to get the notes Great for attendance	The Full-Note Take-in Test (With this type of test, the students must take exacting notes in class. The test is directly from the notes given. The students are allowed to take their own notes into the test—no photocopies of others' work.)	Students may not study Must not lose or have notes stolen Much time spent putting notes on board Notes must be viewed by test supervisor before test

252

123

THE FEAR-OF-PUBLIC-SPEAKING PROBLEM SOLVER

Many English or language arts classes have a public speaking component. It is important for students to develop skills in this area. Sooner or later, most people are called upon to make some sort of presentation to large or small groups of people. This is all fine and dandy, except speaking in public is one of the most feared things for students and adults.

How do you break down that anxiety? The best way is to have experience with it. There's the rub; you can't overcome the fear of public speaking through experience if you are too anxious to start.

FIVE-STEP PROCESS TO BREAK DOWN THE FEAR OF PUBLIC SPEAKING IN STUDENTS

1. Start off by having students read aloud individually from a reader or storybook from their desks.

2. Move the targeted or fearful student to the front desk in the middle row. Continue the individual reading, but have the student you want to help do just a little more than the others.

253

3. At some opportune point, choose to read through a play out loud. While reading, have all the students stand up to read their parts; your targeted student will be at the front, standing up and reading a play part. Continue this until the process becomes routine.

4. At a second opportune time, have students stand up individually to read from a reader or story book, but have the targeted student read slightly more than the others. After this has been repeated a few times, it becomes a natural thing for the fearful student to stand up to read at the front.

5. When the time is right and the targeted student has performed his or her share of standing up and reading, place the child's book on a podium or lectern that faces the class. Presto—the student is speaking in front of the class with a minimum of trauma.

Depending on the student, it may be possible to skip a step or two. The important thing is not to maximize the fear in the student as you teach public speaking skills.

254

TWO DAILY NOTICE OR BULLETIN SYSTEMS FOR QUICK COMMUNICATION

In the process of running a school, announcements must be made to inform students of the various events, programs, and procedures that occur in and around that school. To make the flow of information more efficient, it is a good idea to produce a "daily bulletin." This bulletin should be distributed to each classroom in the morning before school or immediately after lunch break. Several guidelines are important in terms of maximizing the efficiency of this communication tool:

1. You must read the daily bulletin to the students. If a student reads the information, he or she may leave out data he or she thinks is not important. In addition, some students will not listen to other students to the same extent that they will listen to a teacher.

2. A binder with bulletin forms should be available for teachers and students to write information on. This binder of forms should be placed on the office counter or in another convenient location.

3. Once the bulletin deadline has been reached—usually just before school in the morning or afternoon—the information on the bulletin is then photocopied and distributed to each room by a runner, or picked up by teachers before class.

4. The daily bulletin can be referred to any time during the day by students if it is pinned onto the bulletin board. This makes it much more effective than announcements over the intercom, which are heard by only 62 percent of the students—and remembered at a rate of 15 percent or less by those who hear them.

THE DAILY STAFF BULLETIN OR NOTICE

The daily staff notice is very different from the student bulletin. This staff notice is for staff-to-staff communication; it would not normally be distributed to the teachers in the classroom, and is not for access by students.

Some ideas:

1. This staff notice—an interstaff communication system—can contain confidential information about students, such as illnesses, family situations, or problems that the teachers who work with those students must be made aware of.

2. The staff bulletin or notice may contain data about upcoming teacher events, in-services, and so forth.

3. Ideally, this staff notice should be written in a notebook or binder set up for the purpose. This book should be placed on the staff room coffee table, a counter, or a podium set up for the purpose.

4. If this notice or bulletin is placed in a binder or notebook with blank pages for the following days, it becomes possible for a teacher to write the same message as a reminder for an event, for example, on several consecutive days into the future.

5. Staff members can use this bulletin or notice system for the booking of televisions, VCRs, or resource center or computer times—a good way to avoid conflicts and squabbles in these areas.

6. Teachers should be able to add to the staff notice or bulletin any time during the day.

THE COMPREHENSIVE CONTRACT

At the junior high or high school, it can be advantageous to present the whole year's, term's, or semester's required work in a subject area in the form of a contract.

This comprehensive contract lays out the requirements for specific, attainable grade scores for the time frame involved. It states clearly the amount of work required for top marks as well as for lower scores.

You will notice that the sample contract (Figure 5-7) allows for a 10 percent variation within letter grade scores. This is to allow for individual differences in work quality and quantity. You may wish to score Molly at 98 percent in the A+ range and Melissa at 92 percent in the A+ range, because Molly's individual work performance was superior in terms of punctuation, paragraphing, spelling, and so forth.

It should be stressed to students when they sign their contracts and state their targeted grade level that they are making a commitment to perform. Every effort should be made by them to reach the personal goals they have chosen.

You can decide whether to allow contracts to be renegotiated in midterm. This may be advisable in special circumstances; however, too much of a good thing is not so good. If you allow random renegotiation of contracts, this will negate the reason for having the contract in the first place.

SOME ADVANTAGES

1. All students know what amount of work is required to reach a specific grade level.

2. Due dates are clearly marked. This gives students a manageable time frame.

3. Some students need concrete goals in order to perform well. Clear, concise parameters make expectations predictable.

4. Varying degrees of difficulty can be built into the assignments or units of work.

5. If you make some units of work compulsory, you will have students working specifically on areas you want to stress.

Figure 5-7

A SAMPLE OF A COMPREHENSIVE CONTRACT

Time Frame Sept. 3 to Dec. 20
(Semester One)

I hereby agree to do the work required to attain the final grade standing of _____ in English Class.

Work Requirements:

1. To obtain an "A*" (90% to 100%), I will complete 10 of the listed units of work.
2. To obtain an "A" (80% to 89%), I will complete 9 of the listed units of work.
3. To obtain a "B" (70% to 79%), I will complete 8 of the listed units of work.
4. To obtain a "C" (60% to 69%), I will complete 7 of the listed units of work.
5. To obtain a "D" (50% to 59%), I will complete 6 of the listed units of work.

The 10% range within grade scores is to allow for individual differences. A percentage grade will appear as the grade score. Units 1, 3, 5, 8, 9, 10 are compulsory.

Student's Signature _____   Teacher's Signature _____

Units of Work

Unit 1	Unit 2	Unit 3
Prepare an English vocabulary list with the definitions of 50 English grammar terms. Words to seek out are available from the teacher. Due Sept. 15	An 800 word essay on a topic of your choice. Topics must receive prior authorization from the teacher. Due Sept. 30	A 400 word book report or review with at least two character sketches. Due Oct. 7
Unit 4	Unit 5	Unit 6
Create an original work of poetry or prose on a topic of your choice. Due Oct. 15	Present a five minute speech to the class on an approved topic. Due Oct. 27	Prepare a 750 word biography on an "American Hero." Due Nov. 10

Unit 7	Unit 8
Interview an important person in your life or in the area in which you live. Prepare a 300 word question and answer interview. Due Nov. 20	Prepare a 300 word character analysis of Sir John Falstaff from Shakespeare's *Henry IV Part One.* Due Dec. 1
Unit 9	Unit 10
Read a newspaper article on a current topic and write a 300 word editorial on its contents. Due Dec. 10	Prepare an 800 word movie review of a "Golden Oldie" or "Recent Release." Due Dec. 20

126

THE YOUTH COURT SOLUTION

Some strong, wonderfully effective discipline and problem-solving ideas within the structure of society offer a valuable support to schools and school systems. One such program is the youth court/school liaison system at work in the southern part of the province of New Brunswick in Canada.

Operating out of St. John, New Brunswick, this program works with teachers and principals when there is a serious behavior problem at school. This idea enforces the existing laws; no new laws were created for this purpose.

When a problem occurs anywhere within the legal reaponsibility of a school (classroom, travel areas to and from school, school buses, playground, etc.), the teacher or other responsible person first contacts the school principal. The circumstances are detailed there. If the principal deems the problem serious enough, he or she then calls the police, who take statements from all parties concerned. From the police, the information is sent to the Crown (government) lawyer. If that person feels the offense is significant, then court dates are set and the student appears in court. The charge for the offense is then laid against the student in front of the youth court judge. It is only on very rare occasions that the teacher reporting the incident is called upon to testify.

Experience has shown that guilt is proven or admitted in 90 percent or more of the cases. Once a student has pleaded or has been found guilty, he or she is then given a $500.00 fine. The courts do not normally collect or want to collect this money. Students are given 100 hours of community service to perform, and they are allowed to claim a credit of $5.00 for each hour they put in.

Once the community service is finished, the school then decides whether to accept the student back into the classroom. If the student is accepted again, he or she is placed on probation until the end of the current school year. As part of the probationary requirements, the student must complete all assignments, attend school regularly, and obey all school rules.

If a student breaches probation, he or she is then brought by the police or probation officer before the same youth court judge and is often given a night or two of secure custody in a young offenders' lock-up. At this point, other measures are taken to have the student complete his or her sentence requirements. The following is a list of offenses that would cause a charge to be laid against a student:

➠ fighting
➠ theft
➠ willful destruction of property (vandalism)
➠ assaults causing bodily harm
➠ abusive language (telling the teacher "where to go")
➠ threats to teachers
➠ drug use
➠ causing a disturbance

This program in New Brunswick receives excellent support from the youth court system. The judge interviewed personally makes trips to his area schools to explain the program to the students. This, in itself, fosters open communication and helps to prevent problems. It is strongly felt that if students can be informed of this program early enough, it will prevent many offenses from occurring as the children go through the school system.

The main idea behind this program is to help the students recognize that their errant conduct is criminal in nature and cannot be tolerated in the school or any other institution in society.

The important aspect of this idea is accountability. No longer are students just given a slap on the wrist, and then the whole thing forgotten. Students are facing real consequences for real behavior, and it is having a positive ripple throughout the New Brunswick school systems. Behavior problems are at a minimum, and every child can go to school in safety. This helps create that ideal of a positive learning environment.

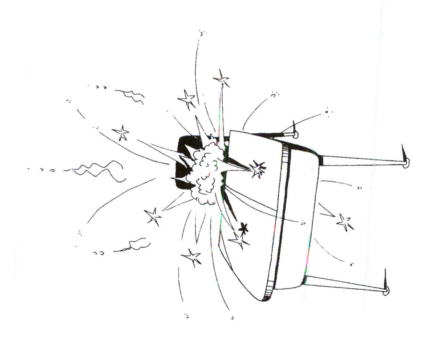

127

POSI-CALLS

Some communication ideas have far-reaching effects in terms of developing positive relationships with parents. A strong relationship is a wonderful asset when it becomes necessary to contact a parent about a situation with his or her child. Posi-calls, or posi-tive phone calls to parents on a regularly scheduled basis, can accomplish wonders.

How It Works and What the Advantages Are

1. Each teacher makes two phone calls a week to parents of students in his or her class-room or homeroom.

2. Target two different students each week and specifically watch for something posi-tive these students have accomplished. It need not be great; lending a pen to anoth-er student is a good example. Describe the positive thing or attitude to the parent during the phone call. A good, communicative conversation with the parent will add to the positive feelings all around.

3. Experience has shown that when a teacher calls a parent, the parent is silent on the other end of the line in the expectation of bad news. When the teacher actually offers positive information, the parent is relieved and often quite grateful. This puts the teacher in a favorable light.

4. If you must, at some time, phone with negative information, this is much more accepted by the parents because you paved the way with positive previous com-munication.

5. If you can get through your whole classroom or homeroom at least once before par-ent-teacher conferences, those conferences will be a much better experience for both you and the parents, as you have introduced yourself in a favorable light.

6. This communication/PR idea has a tremendous mushroom or ripple effect in the community. Parents will talk to parents. The word will get out that you are positive and facilitate open communication.

7. Students feel good about this because they know you will tell their parents about something they did well or about something positive that happened to them at school.

8. In a school of 450 students, with classes of thirty students each, there would be thir-ty phone calls going out each week to thirty-plus parents. It would take fifteen weeks to contact the parents of every student at least once.

9. The posi-calls have to be monitored, so there is no duplication in the calls over the fifteen- to twenty-week period it takes to get through the whole class. The Positive Call Record Sheet (Figure 5-8) has been provided for this purpose.

You will find that these posi-calls are a great asset in establishing positive relation-ships with parents of your students. They open communication on an upbeat note and maintain that level of goodwill throughout the school year. Everyone can surely use this idea; it works well and costs nothing.

Figure 5-8
Positive Call Record Sheet

Name	Date	Home Phone #	Positive Item	Comments

NOTES

NOTES

NOTES

NOTES